CONCISE DICTIONARY OF
PHRASES

A Perfect Reference for Students of all age groups.
Useful guide for aspirants of IAS, CAT, GMAT,
Civil Services, IELTS, TOEFL & Other Examinations

Published by

F-2/16, Ansari Road, Daryaganj, New Delhi-110002
☎ 011-23240026, 011-23240027 • *Fax* 011-23240028
Email info@vspublishers.com • *Website* www.vspublishers.com

Regional Office Hyderabad
5-1-707/1, Brij Bhawan (Beside Central Bank of India Lane)
Bank Street, Koti, Hyderabad - 500 095
☎ 040-24737290
E-mail vspublishershyd@gmail.com

Branch Office Mumbai
Godown # 34 at The Model Co-Operative Housing, Society Ltd.,
"Sahakar Niwas", Ground Floor, Next to Sobo Central, Mumbai - 400 034
☎ 022-23510736
E-mail vspublishersmum@gmail.com

Follow us on

All books available at **www.vspublishers.com**

© Copyright V&S PUBLISHERS
ISBN 978-93-505714-7-7
Edition 2014

The Copyright of this book, as well as all matter contained herein (including illustrations) rests with the Publisher. No person shall copy the name of the book, its title design, matter and illustrations in any form and in any language, totally or partially or in any form. Anybody doing so shall face legal action and will be responsible for damages.

Printed at Param Offseters Okhla New Delhi-110020

Publisher's Note

Considering the growing importance of English in all spheres of life, we recently published an EXC-EL Series (Excellence in English Language) composed of four books - English Vocabulary Made Easy, English Grammar & Usage, Spoken English, and Improve Your Vocabulary. We thought we have done our bit. No sooner, the Series hit the market; a volley of readers sought our help to improve diction, presentation and attractiveness of their conversation – both in writing and speaking.

Being aware that our existence as a publishing house depends solely upon fulfilling readers' expectations and continued patronage, we decided to come out with something that can add spark to any conversation while making it appear interesting. This Dictionary of Phrases is the outcome. There are three more companion dictionaries on – Idioms, Proverbs and Metaphors & Similes.

This book explains the meaning behind hundreds of phrases that you hear or read in English each day. *The meanings are shown in italics.* In order to keep it concise, this dictionary attempts to present most commonly used phrases. Having an exhaustive one will just overwhelm you with thousands of phrases that nobody uses anymore. English remains immensely popular, attractive, articulate and rich language but its phrases are often 'tough nuts to crack'.

What led us to publish this? Phrases appear in every language, and English has thousands of them. They are often confusing because the meaning of the whole group of words taken together has little, often nothing, to do with the meaning of the words taken one by one. In order to understand a language, you must be aware of what the phrases in that language mean. If you try to figure out the meaning of a phrase literally, word by word, you will get completely befuddled.

We would be happy to have your views and comments for improving the content and quality of the edition.

Introduction

What are Phrases?

In everyday speech, a phrase may refer to any group of words. In linguistics, a phrase is a group of words (or sometimes a single word) that form a constituent, and so function as a single unit in the syntax of a sentence. They have a meaning but do not convey the complete meaning. A phrase is lower on the grammatical hierarchy than a clause. A phrase is always a part of a sentence and usually qualifies a Noun or Verb.

Example

The house at the end of the street is red in colour. At the end of the street-Phrase is a list of Phrases with their respective Meanings. Read, understand and learn as many as you can to speak and write better English, and improve as well as enrich your vocabulary.

A

A Bad Egg
Someone/thing that disappoints one's expectations.
A Bed of Roses
An easy situation.
A Bee in Your Bonnet
To be obsessed with something.
A Blot on the landscape
Something that spoils a comfortable situation.
A bolt from the blue
A surprise.
A bun in the oven
To be pregnant.
A bunch of Fives
A fist.
A chip on your shoulder
Keeping a grudge.
A day late and a dollar short
Late and ill prepared.
A different ballpark
Something totally unrelated or of a vastly different scale or scope.
A dime a dozen
When something is extremely simple to obtain.

A dime's worth
An insignificant amount.
A drop in the bucket
An effort or action having very little overall influence, especially as compared to a huge problem.
A drop in the ocean
A very small amount in comparison to the amount that is needed.
A dumb priest never got a parish
Those who fail to speak up fail to get what they want.
A few sandwiches short of a picnic
Exhibiting disquiet or unsoundness of mind; not sane; mad.
A fly in the ointment
Something that creates or introduces an impediment
A fools' paradise
False hopes for a foolish person
A gentleman and a scholar
An admirable person.
A golden key can open any door
Sufficient money can accomplish anything.

A good beginning makes a good ending
Good beginnings promise a good end; start off on a good note to reap the benefits at the end.

A good man is hard to find
Men who make good husbands or workers are rare.

A good voice to beg bacon
Said in ridicule of a bad voice.

A great deal
Very much; to a great extent; a lot; lots.

A house is not a home
A home is not merely a building but requires inhabitants and a friendly atmosphere.

A journey of a thousand miles begins with a single step
Even the longest and most difficult ventures have a starting point

A leopard cannot change its spots
One cannot change one's own nature.

A lie has no legs
You can't get away with a lie, the truth will always come out.

A life of its own
An independent existence with some characteristics of life.

A little bird told me
Of information which was gathered from a source not to be overtly exposed.

A million times
By a factor of a million

A nod is as good as a wink
The hint, suggestion etc can be understood without further explaining.

A notch above
Superior to; of a higher quality than.

A number of
Several of.

A Piece of cake
Something that is simple.

A question of
The important question is; the necessary question is.

A riddle wrapped up in an enigma
Something very mysterious and hidden.

A watched pot never boils
A process appears to go more slowly if one waits for it rather than engaging in other activities.

A wide berth
Wide distance.

Abide by
To accept a decision or law and act in accordance with it; to conform to; to acquiesce; as, to abide by an award.

Abide by
To remain faithful to something or someone; to stand to; to adhere.

Abide with
To remain or live with someone.

Able seaman
Ordinary sailor

Abominable snowman
Yeti

Abound in
To have something in great numbers or quantities; to possess in such abundance as to be characterized by.

Abound with
To have something in great numbers or quantities; to possess in such abundance as to be characterized by.

About time
Close to the right time.

About time
Far past the desired time.

About to
Indicates something that will happen very soon; indicates that something is imminent.

About turn
A complete change of opinion, direction, etc.

About turn
An about face; a military command to a formation of soldiers to reverse the direction in which they are facing.

Above and beyond
More than is expected or required.

Above board
Honestly, reputably.

Above one's bend
Out of one's control or power.

Above the law
Exempt from the laws.

Above the salt
Honorable.

Abstract nonsense
Details which involve unnecessary diagrams.

Abut on
To border on.

Accident of birth
The circumstances around one's birth determine a lot about that person.

Accident waiting to happen
Something which will eventually lead to an accident.

According to
Based on what is said or stated.

Account for
Clarify.

Ace in the hole
A hidden strength.

Ace up one's sleeve
A surprise and hidden advantage..

Ache for
To desire; to want.

Acid test
A hard test searching for the truth.

Acknowledge the corn
To agree to have made a small mistake but not the bigger one.

Across the board
To be relevant to everything.

Across the pond
Referring to the other side of the Atlantic Ocean.

Act like a bull in a china shop
To act rudely in a sensitive situation.

Act on
 To act decisively on something.
Act one's age
 Be mature as your age.
Act out
 To go through a scene; to express one's feelings.
Act up
 Misbehave; cause trouble.
Adams ale
 Water
Add fuel to fire
 To worsen a situation.
Add insult to injury
 To taunt someone after a loss.
Add up to
 Have a particular effect.
Add up
 To sum up; accumulate; make sense.
Adds up
 Enhance.
After all
 In spite of everything.
After one's own heart
 Persons having the same preferences.
After the fact
 After something is finished.
Against all odds
 Despite all difficulties.
Against the clock
 Within a deadline.
Against the collar
 To be in a tight spot.

Against the grain
 Something which is unexpected; unwilling.
Age before beauty
 To allow older people to move before younger ones.
Agree to disagree
 Agreeing to tolerate each individual opinion but not agree to the opinions itself.
Ahead of one's time
 Having something which was expected much later.
Ahead of the game
 Completed a task before it is ready.
Aim at
 Made for a particular audience.
Air bed
 Inflatable mattress
Air out
 Leave out; discuss openly.
Air rage
 Problematic behaviour on an aircraft.
Albatross
 An emotional burden.
Ale post
 A maypole.
All along
 Always.
All and sundry
 Each one.
All and sundry
 Everyone.

All at once
At the same time.
All at once
Unexpected.
All bark and no bite
Talking a lot but not actually acting upon it.
All but
Nearly.
All cats are grey in the dark
Physical appearance is negligible in the dark.
All clear
Permission to go ahead
All duck or no dinner
Everything or nothing.
All ears
Focused and listening.
All ears
Waiting for an explanation.
All eyes and ears
Attentive.
All eyes
Observing attentively.
All fired up
Excited.
All fur coat and no knickers
Superficial appearance with no character.
All good things come to an end
Nothing lasts forever.
All Greek to me
Something that is illegible and can't be understood.
All hell breaks loose
Chaos.

All hollow
A foregone conclusion.
All important
Important
All in a day's work
Dismissal of a significant accomplishment.
All in all
Mostly.
All in
Tired
All it's cracked up to be
As good as reputation would suggest.
All kidding aside
To attempt to make a serious point in a jocular conversation.
All mouth and no trousers
Boastful.
All of a sudden
Suddenly.
All one's eggs in one basket
Investing heavily in just one area.
All out
The state of a side having no more men to bat, ending its innings.
All over but the shouting
The contest is over, but the cheering is still there.
All over grumble
Inferior.
All over hell's half acre
All over the place.
All over the board
Showing a wide range of values with no particular pattern.

All over the map
Widely scattered or distributed.
All over the place
Inconsistent.
All over the shop
Scattered.
All over with
Completely finished.
All over
Finished.
All right, my lover
An affectionate greeting.
All roads lead to rome
Different paths can take one to the same goal
All set
Ready.
All talk and no action
Speaking, promising, or boasting much, but doing little
All talk and no cider
All talk and no results.
All that glitters is not gold
Things that appear valuable might not actually be so.
All that jazz
Other similar things.
All that
Very.
All the marbles
All that is to be had.
All the rage
Very fashionable and popular.
All the same
Nevertheless.

All the tea in china
Something priceless or invaluable.
All the time
Constantly.
All the time
Very often.
All the way to egery and back
The long way.
All things being equal
Without being affected by external factors.
All thumbs
Clumsy.
All to smash
Ruined.
All told
With everything included.
All very well
To a certain extent.
All very well
True.
All walks of life
All professions and lifestyles.
All well and good
Basically good, but with some shortcomings.
All wet
Thoroughly drenched.
All wet
Utterly incorrect.
All work and no play makes jack a dull boy
Too much hard work and not enough leisure time can be unhealthy.
All-a-mort
At death's door.

All-conquering
This is used when you are describing someone or something as better than anyone else.

All-over oneself
Feeling self-satisfied.

Allow for
To take into account when making plans.

Almighty dollar
The dollar satirically characterized as a being a god.

Almost doesn't count
Near success is not deemed success.

Along about
Approximately.

Along the lines
In a general direction.

Also ran
Unplaced horse

Am I right or am I right
Rhetorical question from somebody who has stated what they consider to be a fixed truth.

Amateur hour
A situation or activity in which the participants show a lack of skill, or judgment.

Amber nectar
Lager beer.

An apple a day
Healthy eating and living.

An Arm and a Leg
Something that is extremely costly.

An axe to grind
A grievance, with implications of confrontation.

An englishman's home is his castle
Personal privacy and security is at one's home

An offer one can't refuse
An offer from one side that is so attractive that the other side is guaranteed to accept.

And change
And some quantity.

And counting
Used to show that the number previously mentioned is continuously changing.

And how
Used to strongly confirm preceding utterance.

And shit
Used after a noun or list of nouns in place of "etc".

And so forth
Indicates that a list continues in a similar manner.

And then some
Used to confirm preceding utterance, while implying that what was said or asked is an understatement.

And whatnot
And so on.

Angel's advocate
Someone who sees what's good about an idea and supports it.

Angle for farthings
To beg out of a prison window with

a cap, or box, let down at the end of a long string.

Angle for
To try to obtain something by subtle indirect means.

Another nail in one's coffin
One in a series of factors which lead, or purport to lead, to downfall.

Answer back
To issue echo characters, protocol responses, reflexive connection requests, etc.

Answer back
To reply to a question at a later time.

Answer for
To be held responsible for.

Answer on a postcard
To give a brief answer or opinion.

Anticonstituellement
In french, "I Constantly think you are bugging me, back off or you will regret it."

Any port in a storm
An unfavourable option which might well be avoided in good times but which nevertheless looks better than the alternatives at the current time.

Any press is good press
Being mentioned in the media is beneficial to the subject because it gets publicity.

Any way one slices it
From any perspective.

Anything goes
There are no rules or restrictions.

Apa sambetei
Saturday's waters.

Apple dumplin' shop
A woman's bosom.

Apple of somebody's eye
A favourite, a particular preference, or a loved one; the object of somebody's affections.

Apples and oranges
Said of a comparison of items that are not comparable.

Apply oneself
To put forth a concerted effort; to try; to focus.

Apres-ski
Going out, having drinks, dancing and generally socializing after skiing.

Apron string hold
An estate held by a man during his wife's life.

Are your ears burning
Said of somebody who was not present but was the topic of discussion.

Argue out
To discuss to reach an agreed conclusion, or decision.

Ark ruffian
Rogues who, in conjunction with watermen, robbed, and sometimes murdered, on the water, by picking a quarrel with the passengers in a boat, boarding it, plundering, stripping, and throwing them overboard, etc.

Arm and a leg
A relatively high price for an item or service; an exorbitant price.

Arm candy
An attractive, seemingly romantic companion.

Arm to the teeth
To equip thoroughly with weapons.

Armed forces
The Services.

Armoured car
Military vehicle.

Arm's length
Barely within reach.

Around robin hood's barn
All over the place.

Around the corner
Imminent.

Arrive at
To reach.

Arse about face
Something that is placed or arranged the opposite way to the way it should be.

Arse end of nowhere
A very remote place.

Arse over tit
Tumbling.

Arsy varsey
Tumbling upside down

As a rule
In general; most often.

As a rule
Normally

As all get-out
Extremely; to a superlative degree; very much.

As best one can
In the best possible way, given the circumstances.

As far as one knows
To the best of one's knowledge.

As far as
In the scope of.

As good as one's word
Faithful to a promise one has made.

As if
As though; in a manner suggesting.

As is
In its present state or condition, especially as a contractual condition of sale.

As long as
Depending upon some condition or requirement; provided that; if, assuming; so long as.

As luck would have it
As it happened; how it turned out; by good fortune; fortunately or luckily.

As of
From, on or at a specified time.

As the crow flies
In a straight line distance between two locations, as opposed to the road distance or over land distance.

As well
In addition; also.

As yet
Up to the present; thus far.

Ash Wednesday
First day of lent.

Ask around
To enquire about something to different people.

Ask for it
To provoke an unwanted action.

Ask for the moon
To claim or desire something that one cannot have.

Ask for
Request.

Ask in
To invite someone to enter one's house.

Ask my arse
A common reply to any question; still deemed wit at sea, and formerly at court, under the denomination of selling bargains.

Ask out
To invite somebody, especially on a date.

Ask round
To enquire about something to different people.

Asleep at the switch
Neglectful of an important task, responsibility, or opportunity.

Asphalt jungle
A city or urban area, where the landscape is covered by pavement and the environment is alienating and unsafe.

Ass into gear
Get going; get moving; start producing.

Ass over teakettle
Frantically.

Assault and battery
This legal distinction exists only in jurisdictions that distinguish assault as threatened violence rather than actual violence.

Assume the mantle
To take on a specific role or position, along with any associated responsibilities.

At a glance
Upon cursory examination; an abbreviated review.

At a loss for words
Having nothing to say; stunned to the point of speechlessness.

At a loss
Below the cost or price of purchase.

At a moment's notice
Immediately; instantaneously; without need of warning.

At a pinch
Only just

At a stand
In a state of confusion or uncertainty; undecided what to do next.

At all hours
Late into the night or early morning; when people ought to be sleeping.

At all
Indicating degree, quantity or frequency greater than zero; to

the slightest degree, in any way, somewhat, rather.

At arm's length
At a distance, away from the body.

At bay
Unable to come closer; at a distance.

At best
In the most favourable of conditions; at the most.

At cross purposes
Against one another; contrary in direction or goals.

At death's door
About to die; in a life-threatening state of health.

At ease with nudity
ISM free identification with nude recreation.

At first
Initially; at the start.

At full tilt
At full speed; very quickly.

At hand
Near; soon; approaching; imminent.

At heart
In spirit; according to one's beliefs, views or feelings; deep down, really, fundamentally.

At home
At ease, comfortable.

At large
In general; as a whole.

At last
In the end; finally; ultimately.

At loggerheads
Unable to agree; opposing.

At loose ends
In an uncertain position or situation.

At odds
In disagreement; conflicting.

At once
At the same time; simultaneously; together.

At one with
United with; in tune with.

At one's beck and call
In servitude to; at one's command.

At one's fingertips
Readily available.

At peace with
Not disturbed or upset by.

At peace
Free of worries; peaceful.

At rest
Not moving; stationary.

At risk
Vulnerable

At sea
Confused, lost, or adrift; bewildered.

At sixes and sevens
In a state of confusion.

At stake
In danger; hazarded; pledged; at risk.

At that
In addition to what has been said; furthermore; moreover.

At the best of times
At most.

At the drop of a hat
Without any hesitation; instantly.

At the end of one's tether
At the limit of one's patience; frustrated or annoyed.
At the end of the day
In summary; ultimately.
At the end of the road
No longer in the competition. Voted off. Eliminated.
At the high port
Or in a charge.
At the mercy of
In the power of; defenceless against.
At the moment
Now.
At the ready
Ready; in a state of preparation or waiting; in position or anticipation.
At the top of one's lungs
If you shout at the top your lungs, it means to shout as loudly as you can.
At the wheel
In control of the situation; in charge.
At this point in time
Right now.
At will
At one's preference; as one sees fit.
Au fait
Fully informed.
Auction off
To sell something at an auction.
Autem bawler
A parson.

B

Babe in the woods
A person who is innocent, naive, inexperienced, or helpless.

Babe magnet
A person, especially a man, to whom women are attracted.

Babes in the wood
Criminals in the stocks, or pillory.

Baby blues
Period and feeling of depressiveness after giving birth; a less severe form of postnatal depression.

Baby Father
The father of an infant who is not married to (or is not in a relationship with) the mother.

Back at you
Used to return a greeting.

Back away
Of your attention on the thing in front being avoided.

Back burner
A section of a stove used to keep some pots warm while one focuses on others.

Back down
To take a less aggressive position in a conflict than one previously has or has planned to.

Back gammon player
A sodomite.

Back Handed Compliment
A compliment that also insults someone.

Back in the day
In the past; at one time, especially a time which is fondly remembered.

Back into
To back up or walk backwards and hit something.

Back into
To reverse a vehicle into a space.

Back of beyond
A very remote place.

Back off
To become less aggressive, particularly when one had appeared committed to act.

Back off
To lower the setting of.

Back office
The IT and infrastructure support services for a company, separate from the public face of the business.

Back onto
To overlook something from the rear.

Back out
To withdraw from something one has promised to do.

Back the field
To place a bet on all horses in a race, except one.

Back to basics
To go back to previously held values of decency.

Back to our muttons
To get back to the business at hand.

Back to square one
Back to the beginning.

Back to the drawing board
Back to the beginning following an unsuccessful attempt.

Back up
To provide support or the promise of support.

Back water
A very remote, rural area.

Back-burner
Having low urgency; not currently important.

Back-cloth star
An actor who stands upstage, forcing the other actors to face him and turn their backs to the audience, in order to gain more attention to himself.

Backfoot
To put on the defensive; to put off balance.

Back-of-the-envelope
Approximate, rough, simplified.

Backroom boy
One who is anonymous in an organization while others play more public roles.

Back-seat driver
One who criticizes from the sidelines.

Back-to-back
Identical or similar and sequential.

Bacon fed
Fat, greasy.

Bacon-faced
Having a fat, sleek face.

Bad apple
A person who is not wholesome, honest, or trustworthy, especially one who has an adverse influence on others.

Bad blood
A serious feud or grudge.

Bad egg
Disreputable character

Bad for you
Unhealthy.

Bad hair day
A day on which one's hair seems unmanageable.

Bad iron
Bad luck.

Bad joke
A situation that is badly planned, or illogical.

Bad money drives out good
Debased coinage replaces purer coinage.

Bad penny
A person or thing which is unpleasant, disreputable, or

otherwise unwanted, especially one which repeatedly appears at inopportune times.

Bad taste in one's mouth
A feeling of disappointment and frustration.

Bad to the bone
Completely bad and evil; pure evil.

Badge bunny
A woman who is romantically attracted to police officers and who seeks out their companionship.

Badgered to death
To be tortured and persecuted.

Bag and daggage
All of one's possessions.

Bag of bones
A skinny, malnourished person.

Bag of rations
A fussy or overly zealous military superior.

Bail out on
To abandon, or stop supporting someone or something.

Bail out
To rescue, especially financially.

Baker's dozen
Thirteen of something (one more than a normal dozen).

Balance out
To counteract one another so as to be balanced.

Balance the books
To add up all the debits and credits.

Balancing act
An effort to manage many conflicting or competing items or interests.

Bald eagle
American bird.

Bale out
Alternative spelling of bail out.

Ball and chain
An old slang referring to wife.

Ball up
To hunch over and pull in one's arms and legs.

Ball-breaker
A person or task which is excessively demanding or punishing.

Balloon goes up
Something exciting or dangerous begins.

Ballpark estimate
A ballpark figure, a very rough approximation.

Ballpark figure
An educated guess or estimation within acceptable bounds.

Ballpoint pen
Writing implement.

Balls to the wall
Push to the limit.

Balls-up
Something which becomes muddled or botched in some way.

Balum rancum
A hop or dance, where the women are all prostitutes.

Banana split
Dessert dish

Bandy words with
Argue.

Bang about
To make a lot of percussive noise while doing an activity.

Bang around
To make a lot of percussive noise while doing an activity.

Bang for the buck
Efficiency; cost-effectiveness; value.

Bang on about
To keep talking endlessly about the same subject.

Bang on
Exactly at.

Bang out
To do something quickly, in a slipshod, or unprofessional manner.

Bang straw
A nick name for a thresher, but applied to all the servants of a farmer.

Bang to rights
Caught red-handed; in a guilty state.

Bang up cove
A dashing fellow who spends his money freely.

Bang up job
Something done very well; something performed above average or better than expected.

Bang up
Excellent.

Bang
A loud noise, usually a form of distraction

Banged up
Physically injured or wounded.

Bank night
An event where patrons are enticed to buy entry tickets into some venue.

Bank on
To be sure of something. To depend on it.

Bankers' hours
Any easy job, especially one with a short working day.

Bankers' hours
The period between 10am and 3pm.

Banyan day
In modern usage it refers to a picnic or cookout for the ship's crew.

Baptism by fire
A change in initial attitude or ideals through a traumatic situation.

Baptism of fire
A martyrdom.

Bar fly
A person who frequents bars or lounges to get drunk.

Bar none
Without exception; excluding nothing else of the same kind.

Bar star
A female who frequents bars or lounges, usually late at night.

Bare one's teeth
To show one's aggression.

Barefaced liar
To be shameless.

Barge in
To intrude; to enter or interrupt suddenly and without invitation.
Barge in
To rudely interrupt.
Bark up the wrong tree
To attempt or pursue the wrong thing; to take the wrong approach; to follow a false lead.
Barking mad
Insane.
Barn burner
Any successful or impressive event.
Baron of beef
A large double slice of meat.
Barrel of monkeys
Something very funny or amusing.
Barrow man
A man under sentence of transportation; alluding to the convicts at Woolwich, who are principally employed in wheeling barrows full of brick or dirt.
Base over apex
Falling over in a jumbled heap.
Bash about
To physically damage something or assault someone.
Bash in
To injure someone by hitting violently.
Bash out
To write something very quickly, without much thought.
Bash up
To assault someone with the intention of causing physical injury.

Basket case
One made powerless or ineffective, as by nerves, panic or stress.
Bastardly gullion
A bastard's bastard.
Bat a thousand
To achieve perfection.
Bat an eyelash/eyelid/eye
Slight way; to not show any shock or surprise.
Bat around
To discuss.
Bat away
To avoid by diverting the focus of a discussion.
Bat for both sides
To be a batter for both teams in an amateur baseball game.
Bat for the other team
To be homosexual.
Bated Breath
Breathing slowly and lightly because one is anxious or scared.
Bats in the belfry
To be eccentric.
Batten down the hatches
Prepare for trouble.
Battle cry
Something the troops yell out when going to war or battle.
Battling windmills
Fighting pointless battles.
Bawdy basket
The twenty-third rank of canters, who carry pins, tape, ballads, and obscene books to sell, but live mostly by stealing.

Bawl out
To have a serious argument accompanied with shouting.

Be after
To try to obtain.

Be all ears
To listen carefully or eagerly; to anticipate.

Be along
To arrive.

Be around
To be alive, existent, or present.

Be at one's beck and call
To be in the position of serving someone in any way they desire, usually unwillingly.

Be glad to see the back of
To be glad to get rid of someone; to be glad someone has left.

Be had up
To be accused of, or arrested for a criminal act.

Be in a spot of bother
To have a slight problem, to be in a predicament.

Be in for
To be able to expect or anticipate; to be about to suffer, generally said of something unpleasant.

Be in on
To be a party to a secret shared by a small group of people.

Be left holding the baby
To be left with the responsibility of resolving a problem.

Be mother
To pour out tea for others.

Be my guest
Do as you wish; go ahead; help yourself; go for it.

Be of two minds
To be undecided or unsure; to equivocate; to have multiple opinions.

Be off
To be away from.

Be on about
Talk about; mean, intend.

Be on the edge of one's seat
To be in suspense; to wait eagerly or anxiously for some resolution.

Be on to
To figure out; to realize the truth.

Be still my heart
Calm down, this situation is too exciting or overly distressing.

Be Afraid, be very afraid
A prior warning for an impending danger.

Be still, my beating heart
Expression for excitement.

Be taken ill
To become ill.

Be that as it may
Even if that is the case; whether that is true or not; nevertheless.

Be the way to go
Represent the best of all possible options or courses of action; pre-eminate over all other choices or alternatives.

Be there for
To be available to provide comfort and support for someone, especially in a period of difficulty.

Be there or be square
Used to encourage someone to go somewhere.

Be up against
To be challenged by someone or something stronger than oneself.

Be-all and end-all
Something considered to be of the utmost importance; something essential or ultimate.

Beam up
To be teleported over a long distance by means of a specific imaginary technology, specifically from the surface of a planet to an orbiting starship.

Beam up
To teleport another person or object in the same manner.

Bean feast
A good time.

Bear down on
To approach someone in a very determined way.

Bear down
To press down on someone.

Bear Garden
A state of chaos.

Bear hug
Wrestling hold.

Bear in mind
Remember; consider; note.

Bear in with
Nearer.

Bear on
To influence, have an effect on.

Bear out
To corroborate, prove, or confirm; to demonstrate; to provide evidence for.

Bear up
To endure hardship cheerfully.

Bear with
To be patient with.

Bear witness
Give evidence.

Beast with two backs
Referring to two people engaged in sexual intercourse.

Beat a dead horse
To persist or continue far beyond any purpose, interest or reason.

Beat a hasty retreat
To leave quickly.

Beat about the bush
Avoiding coming to the point.

Beat around the bush
To delay or avoid talking about something difficult or unpleasant.

Beat banaghan
An Irish saying of one who tells wonderful stories, or of something which is amazing and remarkable.

Beat down
To severely beat someone up.

Beat him by a long chalk
Winning over someone in a good way.

Beat it
Go away.

Beat off
To drive something away with blows.

Beat one's head against a stone wall
To waste effort on a futile project.

Beat one's meat
To masturbate.
Beat out
To extinguish.
Beat somebody to the punch
To do something before somebody else is able to.
Beat someone's brains out
To beat someone very severely.
Beat Swords into Ploughshares
To convert to peace instead of war.
Beat the crap out of
To beat really badly.
Beat the living daylights out of someone
To beat up severely.
Beat the rap
Avoid punishment.
Beat up
To feel badly guilty and accuse oneself over something. Usually followed by over.
Beat up
To give a severe beating to.
Beating a dead horse
Something that is pointless.
Beats me
I don't know; I have no idea.
Beauty is only skin deep
What matters is a person's character, rather than his/her appearance.
Beauty is only skin deep
Physical beauty is superficial.
Beauty mark
Or artificially using cosmetics.

Beauty sleep
Extra sleep or a special nap.
Beauty spot
Mole.
Beaver away
To busily undertake a large task.
Because you touch yourself at night
Used to humorously deflect a request for a reason.
Become of
To happen to, to occur to.
Become one flesh
To join together in marriage; to develop a unifying bond as a result of marrying.
Bed down
To put an animal to rest for the night.
Bed of roses
A comfortable or luxurious position.
Beddable
Feminine, great body great legs great taste, trained and beddable, Jesus, how beddable.
Beddy-bye
Bedtime for a toddler, going to sleep, going to bed.
Bee in one's bonnet
Something of particular interest or concern; an obsession.
Beef about something
To complain.
Beef and reef
A cuisine that combines both meat and seafood.

Beef to the hoof
Fat, chubby, particularly with fat legs.
Beefed out
Muscular, often in an exaggerated way.
Been there, done that
An assertion that the speaker has personal experience or knowledge of a particular place or topic and is now bored.
Been to the rodeo
Exposed to conmen and hucksters; experienced.
Beer and skittles
Fun times.
Beer goggles
The illusion that people are more attractive, brought on by alcohol consumption.
Bee's knees
Something excellent, outstanding.
Beetle-browed
To have a worried expression.
Before you can say jack robinson
Very quickly. Quicker than you expect.
Beg off
To avoid, or cancel some event that one has previously arranged with someone.
Beg to differ
To differ strongly in opinion or interpretation.
Behind bars
In jail or prison.
Behind closed doors
Public disclosure.

Behind every great man there's a great woman
A woman is always responsible for a man's success.
Behind its time
Showing characteristics of the past; present in one's work after later advances in the field; coming later than could be generally accepted.
Behind somebody's back
Without somebody's knowledge; secretly.
Behind the bit
An equestrian term, meaning that the horse is evading the bit.
Behind the counter
Of drugs, dispensed by a pharmacist without needing a doctor's prescription or other form of compliance.
Behind the eight ball
A difficult position from which one can't probably escape.
Behind the scenes
In secret; out of public view.
Believe in
To ascribe existence to.
Believe you me
An emphatic form of "believe me".
Bell, book and candle
To be excommunicated from the Catholic church.
Bells and whistles
Extra features added for show rather than function; fancy additions or features.

Belly up
Dead or defunct.

Below par
Having a price below its face value.

Below the belt
An unfair and hidden move.

Below the salt
Something which is common.

Belt and braces
To be careful and not take risks.

Belt and suspenders
Redundant systems, affording mutual backup in the event of one failing.

Belt up
Be quiet.

Bench jockey
A baseball term for a player, coach or manager who is annoying and distracts opposition players and umpires from his team's dugout bench with verbal repartee.

Bend one's elbow
To drink alcoholic beverages, especially at a public house or bar.

Bend over backwards
To make a great effort; to take extraordinary care; to go to great lengths.

Bend somebody's ear
To bore; to talk too long.

Bend the truth
To change or leave out certain facts of a story or situation, generally in order to elicit a specific response in the audience.

Bent on a splice
About to be married.

Bent on
Completely determined; obstinate.

Beside oneself
Overcome; consumed by an emotion.

Beside the point
Irrelevant, moot.

Best bet
The best proposal or plan.

Best Bib and Tucker
Best clothes.

Best laid plans
A proverbial expression used to signify the futility of making detailed plans when the outcome is uncertain.

Best laid schemes of mice and men
Sometimes one's most carefully and well planned plans may go wrong.

Best of both worlds
A combination of two seemingly contradictory benefits.

Best of the bunch
The best or most preferred person or item within a group.

Best regards
Used as a polite closing of a letter.

Bet dollars to donuts
To suggest that something is very likely to be true or that one has a strong hunch about something.

Bet the farm
To be absolutely certain, to have no doubts.

Bet your bottom dollar
To bet one's last coin.

Better an egg today than a hen tomorrow
It is better to have a sure thing now than a possibility of more later.

Better half
A person's lover.

Better safe than sorry
It is preferable to be cautious in one's choices and actions than to suffer afterwards.

Better than sex
Wonderful.

Between a rock and a hard place
To be faced with two choices in a difficult situation.

Between the jigs and the reels
Eventually, despite all the confusion.

Between you, me and the bed-post
Referring to a secret about which only the speaker and listener should know.

Betwixt and between
Neither one thing nor the other.

Beware of Greeks bearing gifts
One shouldn't trust one's enemies.

Beyond one's pay grade
Beyond one's capability.

Beyond our ken
Beyond one's understanding.

Beyond the black stump
Extremely remote, outside the populated area.

Beyond the pale
Socially unacceptable.

Big boys
The people or bodies with the most influence and/or power.

Big break
A breakthrough, especially the first big hit of a previously unknown performer or performers in the entertainment industry.

Big bucks
Lots of money.

Big cheese
A very important figure, especially a high-ranking person in an organization.

Big daddy
Something or someone of importance.

Big deal
Something very important, difficult, or of concern.

Big enchilada
A very important person, especially the highest-ranking individual in an organization.

Big enchilada
Some item of high value, especially a top prize or reward.

Big fat
Complete, utter, total.

Big fish in a small pond
One who has achieved a high rank or is highly esteemed, but only in a small, relatively unimportant, or little known location or organization.

Big gun
Someone who is powerful or influential most often in plural form.

Big kahuna
A boss, leader, chieftain, or top-ranking person in an organization.

Big mouth
The mouth of someone who talks too much, especially by making exaggerated claims or by inappropriately revealing information.

Big picture
The totality of a situation.

Big shot
A person with a reputation of importance or power.

Big sleep
Death.

Big top
Circus tent.

Big up
To proclaim or exaggerate the importance of.

Big wheel
A person with a great deal of power or influence, especially a high-ranking person in an organization.

Big wig
One who is important in their field.

Bigger fish to fry
A higher valued result or target to reach.

Big wig
A person of importance to a group or organization.

Bill of goods
A set of misleading or deceptive claims; misinformation.

Billy no-mates
A person with no friends.

Binge drinking
Drinking too much in a little time.

Bird in the bosom
A secret pledge that one makes for another.

Bird of one's own brain
One's own idea or conception.

Birds and bees
Informal sex education, especially describing the sexual activity of animals rather than that of people.

Birds of a feather
People having similar characters, backgrounds, interests, or beliefs.

Bird's-eye view
The view from directly or high above.

Birthday suit
Nakedness; a lack of clothing.

Bit by a barn mouse
Tipsy.

Bit on the side
Secondary lover, mistress.

Bit part
Small acting role.

Bite i gresset
To bite the dust, to die.

Bite me
An expression of discontent or aggravation to another party.

Bite of the reality sandwich
A wake-up call, a reality check.

Bite off more than one can chew
To try to do too much; to take on or attempt more than one is capable of doing.

Bite one's tongue
An admonishment to someone who has said something unfeeling or harsh.

Bite someone's head off
To severely berate someone.

Bite the bullet
To endure a punishment or consequence with dignity or stoicism.

Bite the dust
To fall down- wounded or dead.

Bite the hand that feeds you
To cause harm to a benefactor.

Bite to eat
A snack or quick meal.

Bite your tongue
Be quiet.

Bits and bobs
A random assortment of things; small remaining pieces and things.

Bitter end
That part of an anchor cable which is abaft the bitts and thus remains onboard when a ship is riding at anchor.

Bitter end
The end of a long and difficult process.

Bitter pill
Something unpleasant that must be accepted or endured.

Black and blue
Covered in bruises.

Black babies
Third world charities, the missions.

Black ball someone
A person who is not acceptable in a group.

Black magic
Magic derived from evil forces, as distinct from good or benign forces; or magic performed with the intention of doing harm.

Black maria
Police van

Black sheep of the family
A person who doesn't conform to one's family's rules and ideals.

Black sheep
A disliked person.

Black
Bad; evil.

Black-on-black
Something that is invisible or intentionally obfuscated, such as warnings or fine print.

Blame canada
A catch phrase for shifting attention away from a serious social issue by laying responsibility with Canada.

Blanket term
A word or phrase that is used to describe multiple groups of related things.

Blast from the past
Something/one from the past.

Blast off
To begin

Blaze a trail
To show the way or proceed rapidly.

Blaze a trail
Lead the way.

Bleed like a stuck pig
To bleed heavily.

Bleeding edge
Something very current.

Bleep out
To censor inappropriate spoken words by obscuring them with the sound of a bleep.

Blessed event
An occurrence or occasion which is particularly noteworthy and enjoyable.

Blessing in disguise
A misfortune that has an unexpected benefit.

Blimp out
To become fat or fatter, especially as a result of excessive eating.

Blind as a bat
Nearly totally blind, having a very poor sense of vision.

Blind date
A romantic meeting between two people who have never met before.

Blind leading the blind
Situation where an unqualified person is attempting to train others in a task.

Blind
Any device intended to conceal or hide; as, a duck blind.

Bling-bling
Referring to over-the-top clothes or jewellery.

Blink of an eye
A very short period of time; quickly.

Blonde bombshell
Referring to a beautiful blonde.

Blood is thicker than water
Family relations and loyalties are stronger than relationships with people who are not family members.

Blood mary
Vodka and tomato juice

Bloody-minded
Stubborn.

Blot one's copy book
To damage one's own reputation through bad behavior.

Blot out
To obscure.

Blow a fuse
To lose one's temper; to become enraged.

Blow a gasket
To become very angry or upset.

Blow a kiss
To kiss one's hand, then blow on the hand in a direction towards the recipient.

Blow away
Flabbergast; scintillate; impress greatly.

Blow chunks
To be very bad, inadequate, unpleasant, or miserable; to thoroughly suck.

Blow hot and cold
To behave inconsistently; to vacillate or to waver, as between extremes of opinion or emotion.

Blow it
To fail at something; to mess up; to make a mistake.

Blow off some steam
To enjoy oneself.

Blow off steam
To rant or shout in order to relieve stress; to vent.

Blow off
To shoot something with a gun, causing it to come disconnected.

Blow one's chances
To forfeit opportunities to achieve some goal.

Blow one's top
To be explosively angry. To lose one's temper.

Blow out of proportion
To overreact to or overstate; to treat too seriously or be overly concerned with.

Blow over
To pass naturally; to go away; to settle or calm down.

Blow smoke
To speak with a lack of credibility, sense, purpose, or truth; to speak nonsense.

Blow someone out of the water
To trounce; to defeat someone thoroughly, at a game or in battle.

Blow someone's mind
To astonish someone, to flabbergast someone.

Blow the gaff
Reveal a secret.

Blow the whistle
To disclose information to the public.

Blow this pop stand
To exit or remove oneself from a less than exciting location or environment.

Blow this popsicle stand
To leave an establishment speedily.

Blow up in one's face
To fail disastrously.

Blow up
To fail disastrously.

Blow your mind
To be surprised by something/one.

Blow your own trumpet
To be boastful.

Blow-by-blow
Detailing every action or occurrence completely.

Blowing smoke
To boast without any proof.

Blue blood
Referring to the blood of aristocratic families.

Blue devils
Low spirits; depression.

Blue note
Notes added to the major scale for expressive quality in jazz and blues music, particularly the flatted third, fifth and seventh.

Blue wash
To tout a business or organization's commitment to social responsibility.

Blue-eyed boy
Someone's favourite, especially a young one.

Blue-plate special
A set meal at a less price.

Blurt out
To say suddenly, without thinking.

Bo jook
Bluffing.

Board up
To block doors or windows with

boards, either to prevent access or as protection from storms, etc.

Bob is your uncle
Meaning that everything is fine.

Bodice ripper
A sexually explicit romantic novel.

Body surfing
Surfboarding.

Bog standard
Especially plain, ordinary, or unremarkable; having no special, excess or unusual features; plain vanilla.

Bog Standard
A raw material.

Bogged down
Stuck.

Boil down to
To be equivalent to; to reduce to.

Boil down
As an allusion to the cooking technique of reducing liquids by heat, one boils down a problem, argument, etc. to its most central elements.

Bolt bucket
A machine, especially an automobile. Implies that the machine is clunky or unreliable.

Bomb around
The drive around at speed for pleasure.

Bone dry
Completely dry; without any trace of moisture.

Bone Idle
Lazy.

Bone of contention
Something that continues to be disputed; something on which no agreement can be reached.

Bone up on
Study hard.

Bone up
To study or cram, especially in order to refresh one's knowledge of a topic.

Boo boo
Blunder.

Booby prize
A prize for a loser of a game.

Booby trap
A practical joke.

Boogie-woogie
A style of blues music, linked to jazz.

Book in
Register.

Boot camp
Any short, intensive course of training.

Boot camp
A basic training program.

Boot is on the other foot
Circumstances being reversed.

Boot up
To start a computer using its bootstrap procedure.

Bootleg liquor
Illegal liquor.

Booze can
A nightclub or bar, especially one which operates illegally or is otherwise disreputable.

Borganism
Forms of government.

Born in a barn
Engaging in the behaviour of leaving open a door or window.

Born in a barn
Ill-mannered.

Born with a silver spoon in one's mouth
Born to a wealthy family.

Born with a silver spoon in one's mouth
Born into a rich family.

Born yesterday
New and inexperienced.

Borne out
Confirm.

Boss about
To boss around; behave dominantly, ordering everyone around.

Boss-eyed
Cross-eyed.

Botch a job
To repair badly.

Bottle out
To fail to perform something due to fright.

Bottom line
Result.

Bottom of the barrel
The least desirable.

Bottom of the line
The worst.

Bottom of the ninth
Last opportunity.

Bottoming the house
Cleaning one's house from top to bottom.

Bottoms up
Drinking something in one go.

Bought the farm
Died.

Bought the farm
To die.

Bounce back
To restart after a negative occurrence.

Bouncing off the walls
Moving hyperactively.

Bow out
To leave with one's credibility still intact.

Bowl a googly
Something unexpected.

Bowl a maiden over
To tremendously impress a woman.

Bowl of cherries
An enjoyable experience.

Bowl out
End of innings.

Bowl over
To flabbergast.

Bowled over
Surprised

Box and Cox
To cut and change.

Box on the ear
To hit someone on the ear to enforce attention.

Box the compass
To make a complete reversal.

Box Your Ears
To beat up someone.

Boxer shorts
Underwear

Box-office bomb
A motion picture that generates relatively low revenue at the box office.

Boys and their toys
Used to evoke the idea that adult men sometimes dote excessively on machines, automobiles, and gadgets in a childish manner.

Boys will be boys
It is hard, often fruitless, to attempt to curb the natural playfulness and tendency to mischief of most growing boys.

Brace of shakes
A very short time.

Bragging rights
The prerogative to praise oneself for an accomplishment or for possession of a superior characteristic.

Brain fart
Something ill-considered and said or done impulsively.

Brain surgeon
Someone very intelligent.

Brain surgery
Something that is overly complex, detailed or confusing.

Brain teaser
Puzzle

Brain-dead
Having no useful thoughts; stupid; ditzy.

Branch out
To attempt something new or different, but related.

Brand spanking new
Completely new.

Brass farthing
Something worthless or of small value.

Brass neck
Shamelessness.

Brass ring
Figuratively, a prize or goal.

Brass-necked
Nervy; cheeky; shameless.

Bread and butter
That which is central or fundamental, as to one's business, survival, or income; a staple or cornerstone.

Breadwinner
The member of a household who earns all or most of the income.

Break a leg
A wish for a successful performance; primarily a valediction to an actor wishing him or her a successful theatrical stage performance.

Break A Leg
Said to wish someone good luck.

Break a sweat
To put effort into something.

Break away
To leave suddenly.

Break down
To fail.

Break even
To stay the same; to neither advance nor regress.

Break ground
To initiate a new venture, or to advance beyond previous achievements.

Break in the case
A new discovery in a case.
Break in
To enter by force or illicit means.
Break into
To enter illegally or by force.
Break new ground
To initiate a new venture.
Break off
To end abruptly, either temporarily or permanently.
Break one's duck
To do something for the first time.
Break out
To escape, especially forcefully or defiantly.
Break rank
To march or charge out of the designated order in a military unit.
Break someone's heart
To cause a person to feel grief or sadness.
Break the back of
To achieve the greater part of some project.
Break the bank
To exhaust one's financial resources.
Break the buck
Fall below the value of one dollar per share.
Break the ice
To start to get to know people, by avoiding awkwardness.
Break up
To break or separate into pieces; to disintegrate or come apart.

Break wind
To be flatulent.
Break your back
Definition to work extremely hard
Breakfast of champions
An ironic appellation for beer, junk food, or other foods implied to be unhealthy.
Breath of fresh air
Something relieving, refreshing, or new.
Breathe down someone's neck
To follow someone too closely, making it uncomfortable for them.
Breathe easy
To relax or feel secure about something.
Brick by brick
To create or build something in a steady, step-by-step fashion.
Brick up
To block by masonry, particularly using bricks.
Brick wall
An obstacle.
Brickbat
A criticism or uncomplimentary remark hurled at artwork or other recipient.
Bricks and clicks
A sales model that uses both traditional stores and Internet selling.
Bridge
A statement, such as an offer, that signals a possibility of accord.

Bright line
A clear distinction in the context of a legal or moral judgment.
Brighten up
To make cheerful.
Bright-eyed and bushy-tailed
Alert and in an eager, frisky, or playful mood; full of life.
Bright-line rule
A clear-cut, easy to make decision.
Brim over
To overflow over the brim.
Bring about
To accomplish, achieve.
Bring back
To cause someone to remember something from the past.
Bring down the house
To garner enthusiastic or wild applause.
Bring down
To reduce.
Bring forth
To display, produce, bring out for display.
Bring forward
To call up for consideration.
Bring home the bacon
To have a job and earn money or to lead a successful career.
Bring in
To introduce a person or group of people to an organisation.
Bring it on
Used to indicate one's willingness to accept a challenge, confront a threat, etc.

Bring it weak
To fail to accomplish an accomplishable task or to make an attempt at less than maximum effort; to "half-ass" or "fake the funk".
Bring off
To succeed in doing something considered to be very difficult.
Bring out
To elicit, evoke, or emphasize a particular quality.
Bring owls to athens
To undertake a pointless venture, one that is redundant, unnecessary, superfluous, or highly uneconomical.
Bring round
To bring something when coming.
Bring to heel
To be forced to obey.
Bring to the table
To provide a suggestion.
Bring up
To bring from a lower position to a higher position.
Bring upon
To cause to befall.
Broad across the beam
Without fat on the hips and the bottom.
Broad church
A wide scope of philosophies and ideas.
Broad in the beam
Having wide hips.
Broad shoulders
The ability to take criticism, or accept responsibility.

Broken vessel
A person who is destroyed or forgotten, or who feels flawed or broken.

Broken-hearted
Feeling depressed, despondent, or hopeless, especially over losing a love.

Bros before hoes
A man should prioritize his male friends over his girlfriend or wife.

Brown bag
A short presentation or seminar on a given subject, especially one given at lunchtime.

Brown bread
Bread with a brown colour as distinct from white bread, wholemeal, granary or other specific types of bread.

Brown noser
One who sucks up; a bootlicker, ass-kisser, sycophant.

Brown nosing
To be overly nice so as get into the good books of one's superiors.

Brown power
The production of electricity made from conventional sources, such as coal, oil, natural gas and nuclear power.

Brown thumb
Lack of skill at growing plants; something possessed by a poor gardener.

Browned off
Annoyed, upset, angry, bored, fed up, disgusted.

Brownie points
Marks of achievement.

Brummagem screwdriver
A type of hammer.

Brush off
An abrupt rebuff or dismissal.

Brush up
To review; to improve an existing but rusty or under-developed skill.

Bubble and squeak
A dish consisting of fried potatoes and other vegetables.

Buck off
To cause to fall off.

Buck up
Hurry up; make haste.

Bucket down
To rain heavily.

Bucket of bolts
A piece of machinery that is not worth more than its scrap value, often of old cars.

Buckle down
To put forth the needed effort; to focus; become serious; apply oneself.

Buckle down
Work hard.

Buckle up
To fasten one's seat belt or safety belt.

Bud
A mate, a friend

Bug off
Used to tell somebody to leave them alone.

Bug out
   To abandon someone without warning.
Bugger all
   Nothing.
Bugger off
   Go away.
Bugger up
   To break or spoil something, or make it inoperative, useless etc.
Build a better mousetrap
   To invent the next great thing; to have a better idea.
Build up
   To accumulate, to pile up.
Built like a brick shithouse
   Exceptionally well constructed; strong or tough.
Built like a tank
   Broad shouldered and of solid, muscular build.
Bull session
   An informal meeting among men.
Bulletproof
   Unbreakable, very tough.
Bull's eye
   Sweet
Bum around
   To wander around idly to no purpose; to loaf or loiter.
Bum chum
   A male's homosexual partner.
Bum rap
   An undeservedly unfavorable portrayal or reputation.
Bum rush
   Storming into an establishment.

Bum steer
   Bad advice, regardless of intention.
Bump and grind
   A combination of movements.
Bump and grind
   A sexually suggestive dance involving exaggerated hip movements, especially a striptease dance.
Bump into
   To meet someone by chance.
Bump off
   To kill, especially to murder.
Bump up
   To increase something suddenly.
Bumper crop
   A large yield; an excess of something.
Bumpy
   To become upset.
Bums on seats
   Refers to the paying audience at a theatre or cinema.
Bundle of energy
   One who is especially lively, continually active, or industrious.
Bundle of joy
   A newborn baby.
Bundle of nerves
   A person with an especially nervous, excitable, or fearful disposition.
Bung up
   To close an opening with a cork, cork like object or other improvised obstruction.
Bunk off
   To play truant.

Bunny boiler
An obsessive and often dangerous female.
Bunny hop
A ground ball that hops along the field instead of rolling.
Bunny hug
A style of dance.
Buoy up
To uplift, hearten, inspire or raise the spirits.
Buried treasure
Something, having been concealed for a long time, which later is found and is profitable.
Burn a hole in one's pocket
To cause someone to be tempted to spend money.
Burn down
To completely burn, so that nothing remains.
Burn one's bridges
To destroy one's path, connections, reputation, opportunities, etc.
Burn one's candle at both ends
To work extremely or excessively hard; to work too hard for good health or peace of mind.
Burn one's fingers
To harm oneself; to suffer consequences of one's actions.
Burn out
To tire due to overwork.
Burn rubber
To accelerate so rapidly from standstill that it leaves a mark of burnt rubber on the road from the tire.

Burn the midnight oil
To work studiously, especially late into the night.
Burn up
To anger; to annoy.
Burning the midnight oil
To work late at night.
Burnt to a crisp
Inedible.
Burst someone's bubble
To disillusion.
Bury the hatchet
To settle one's differences with an enemy.
Bury the lead
To begin a story with details of secondary importance to the reader while postponing more essential points or facts.
Bury your head in the sand
To refuse to confront problem.
Bush league
A low-ranking or inferior level among groups, professions, organizations, etc.
Bush telegraph
A gossip network.
Business as usual
The normal course of an activity, particularly in circumstances that are out of the ordinary.
Business before pleasure
An admonishment that discharging one's obligations must take precedence over devoting time to pursuits meant solely for one's own gratification.

Business end
The part of a tool or other similar item, that is physically used for its operation, rather than the part which is held.

Business girl
A prostitute.

Busman's holiday
A holiday or vacation during which you do the same thing that you do for your usual work.

Bust a cap in someone's ass
Alternative form of pop a cap in someone's ass.

Bust ass cold
Extremely cold.

Bust chops
To nag; to berate or hound in an effort to elicit action.

Bust one's butt
To work exceptionally hard.

Bust one's chops
To exert oneself.

Bust your balls
To harass so as to completely brake someone's spirits.

Busted flush
Anything which ends up worthless despite great potential.

Busting your chops
To say something to harass someone.

Bustle with
To teem with; abound with; to exhibit an energetic and active abundance of a thing; to be full of a certain activity or active beings.

Busy beaver
Someone who is very busy or hard-working.

Busy work
Work or activity performed with the intention or result of occupying time.

But seriously folks
Directs attention to immediately preceding failed attempt at humor.

But then
Then again, on the other hand; used to show that the opposite viewpoint is possible.

But who's counting
Used as a retort or comeback, often to deprecate oneself or another for excessive concern or attention to.

Butt heads
To argue uncompromisingly with someone.

Butt of a joke
The person who comes out ridiculed when a story is told.

Butter fingers
A clumsy person who always drops things, a klutz.

Butter up
To flatter, especially with the intent of personal gain.

Butter wouldn't melt in his mouth
A prim and proper person.

Butterfly upon a wheel
An innocent person crushed by life's adversities.

Butt-naked
Stark-naked, completely nude.

Button up
To fasten with a button or buttons.

Button-down
Conservative; conventional; unimaginative.

Buttoned-down
Alternative form of button-down.

Buy a pig in a poke
To buy something without checking it.

Buy out
To purchase the entire stock or extent of something.

Buy straw hats in winter
Of stocks, to buy when both demand and price is low, sell when demand and price is high.

Buy the farm
To die; often, to die in battle.

Buy time
Purposefully cause a delay to something, in order to achieve something else.

Buy to let
To purchase a property as in investment, and to let it out for rental instead of living in it.

Buzz off
Used to tell someone to go away.

Buzz up
To allow entrance into a building from a higher floor by triggering an electronic lock.

By a long shot
By a wide margin; indicates a very big difference or disparity.

By all means
Yes certainly; definitely.

By and large
Mostly, generally; with few exceptions.

By and large
On the whole.

By dint of
By reason of; by means of.

By far
To a considerably large extent, easily.

By george
An expression used to express surprise.

By gum
Surprise.

By hand
Manually; without the use of automation or machines.

By heart
Knowing completely; as having committed completely to memory.

By hook or by crook
By any means, whether fair or unfair.

By leaps and bounds
Rapidly. Said of making progress.

By no means
Certainly not; definitely not.

By one's lights
According to one's understanding.

By one's own hand
As a result of one's own actions, especially with reference to death by suicide.

By oneself
Alone; without assistance, accompaniment, or help from others.

By the book
In a manner which adheres strictly to rules, legal requirements, or official procedures.

By the Book
According to the rules.

By the by
Used to introduce a new topic; incidentally.

By the grace of god
By divine right.

By the numbers
To do something exactly, precisely, or in a formulaic way.

By the same token
For a similar reason; in a similar manner; similarly; likewise; along the same lines.

By the short hairs
To be trapped by an opponent in an inescapable position.

By the skin of one's teeth
Barely; closely; by a narrow margin; with nothing to spare.

By the skin of your teeth
A narrow escape from disaster.

By the time
When.

By the way
Incidentally; a parenthetical statement not timely, central, or crucial to the topic at hand; foregone, passed by, something that has already happened.

By trade
As a profession; professionally.

By virtue of
Because of; on the grounds of; by reason of; due to; based on.

Bye-bye
Goodbye.

By-the-book
Adhering strictly to rules, legal requirements, or official procedures.

By-the-numbers
Done in a predictable manner; formulaic.

C

Cake crumbs
Hardly anything.

Call a spade a spade
To speak the truth; to say things as they really are.

Call 'em as one sees 'em
To candidly and honestly express an opinion or viewpoint.

Call forth
To induce, inspire.

Call in
To summon.

Call it a day
To retire.

Call it even
To declare debts resolved or favors or other exchange equitable.

Call it quits
To conclude; to quit or stop an activity.

Call off the dogs
To ease up on after inflicting great punishment.

Call off
To recall; to cancel or call a halt to.

Call on
To visit somebody; to pay a call.

Call out
To specify, especially in detail.

Call someone's bluff
To take action on the basis that another person is bluffing.

Call the shots
To make the decisions; to be in charge; to give orders.

Call up
An order to report for military service.

Called on the carpet
To be held accountable for a mistake, offense, or a lie.

Calling card
An attribute, object, or behavior which is distinctly characteristic of someone or something.

Calls for
Requires; needs to

Camel through the eye of a needle
Almost impossible to do or to happen.

Camel's nose
A situation where the permitting

of some small act will lead consequently to a larger undesirable act or circumstance.

Can it
To silence; to quit doing something; to put an end to something.

Can it
Stop what you are doing or saying.

Can of worms
A complex, troublesome situation arising when a decision or action produces considerable subsequent problems.

Cancel out
To neutralize the effect of something.

Cannon fodder
Military personnel who are regarded as expendable when attacking the enemy.

Can't get a word in edgewise
Unable to break into a conversation, no pause in a discussion.

Can't hold a candle to
To be far less competent or have far less skills than someone else.

Can't wait
To eagerly anticipate; to find it unbearable to wait for a forthcoming pleasurable event.

Cap it all off
To finish or complete something.

Cap off
To finish.

Cap over the windmill
In a crazed manner.

Captain of industry
A prominent business person who owns or is the highest-ranking executive of one or more major firms.

Carbon copy
Duplicate

Carpe diem
Seize the day, make the most of today, enjoy the present

Carried away
Made excessively emotional or excited.

Carrot and stick
Simultaneous rewards for good behavior and punishments for bad behavior.

Carry a torch for
To harbor feelings of love despite not being in a relationship.

Carry a tune
To produce music, especially to sing, with accurate pitch.

Carry away
To break under sudden pressure of violent wind.

Carry coals to newcastle
To do something that is unneeded or redundant.

Carry off
Knowledge, confidence, or familiarity.

Carry on
To act or behave; especially to act or behave so as to attract attention.

Carry one's weight
To contribute or produce one's fair share, as of work, money, etc.

Carry out
To fulfill.

Carry someone's water
To do someone's bidding; to serve someone's interests.

Carry the can
To take the blame for something in which others have also taken part and are largely responsible.

Carry the message to garcia
To perform a requisite task despite obstacles.

Carry water for
To perform menial tasks for; to serve; to assist.

Carved in stone
Unchangeable.

Case in point
An example that illustrates a point.

Cash cow
A product, service, or enterprise that generates ongoing, high net free cash flows.

Cash in
To profit from; to use an opportunity to maximum advantage, especially financially.

Cast aspersions
To make damaging or spiteful remarks.

Cast away
To discard.

Cast off
To discard or reject something.

Cast on
To start the first row of knitting by putting stitches on a needle.

Cast one's vote
To vote for something.

Cast pearls before swine
To give things of value to those who will not understand or appreciate it.

Cast the first stone
To act self-righteously in accusing another person, believing that one is blameless.

Cast up one's accounts
To vomit.

Castle in the air
A visionary project or scheme; a day-dream; an idle fancy; a pipe dream; any plan, desire, or idea that is unlikely to be ever realized; a near impossibility.

Cat and dog life
Unhappy married life.

Cat and mouse game
Two individuals and/or groups repeatedly keeping check on each other in a suspicious or self-protective way, often with the goal of one or both parties trying to gain a malicious advantage over the other.

Cat got someone's tongue
Means why are you not saying anything?

Cat in the meal-tub
Something concealed; a hidden danger.

Cat in the sack
Something to be suspicious of.

Cat that ate the canary
A person who appears self-satisfied or smug, especially while concealing something mischievous, prohibited, or private.

Catbird seat
Expression used to describe an enviable position, often one of great advantage.

Catch 22
A no win situation - one where, whatever happens, there will almost certainly be a bad outcome.

Catch a buzz
To become slightly inebriated, but not yet be drunk.

Catch a cold
To become infected with cold.

Catch a tan
To get a suntan.

Catch air
To make a jump.

Catch big air
Superlative of catch air; make a big jump high off the ground.

Catch dust
To be rarely used.

Catch fire
Become engulfed with flames.

Catch flies
An ostensible product of awkwardly having one's mouth open wide.

Catch hell
Be severely reprimanded, punished, or beaten.

Catch it
Be severely reprimanded, punished, or beaten.

Catch on
To begin to understand; to realize or detect.

Catch out
To discover or expose as fake or insincere.

Catch some Z's
To sleep.

Catch someone's eye
To capture someone's attention.

Catch up
To pick up suddenly.

Catch-as-catch-can
Intermittent; only when possible or when the opportunity presents itself.

Catmeat
Someone who has been badly beaten.

Cat's cradle
Any complicated structure which appears to be without purpose.

Cat's meow
A self-satisfied person.

Cat's pyjamas
That new car was really the cat's pyjamas.

Cattle call
An audition which is open to the public and thus draws a large number of applicants, many of whom are inexperienced.

Caucus race
A political competition; the game of

campaigning and one-upmanship to get votes and be elected.

Caught between the devil and the deep blue sea
Having a choice between two alternatives, both undesirable.

Caught eavesdropping
A person found to be deliberately trying to overhear a conversation not intended for his/her ears.

Caught in the act
To be found doing something that you weren't supposed to be doing, while you're doing it.

Caught Red-Handed
Caught in the act.

Caught with his pants down
Finding oneself in an awkward, unexpected and uncompromising situation.

Caught with one's hand in the cookie jar
Observed or apprehended while committing a theft, especially while embezzling money.

Caught with one's pants down
Caught off guard, unprepared, or in an embarrassing situation.

Cause a stir
To cause controversy, or raise a disturbance.

Cave in
The act of relenting.

Caveat lector
Reader beware.

Cease fire
Truce.

Cease to be
To die.

Center field
A central role in some activity that requires speed.

Centre half
Footballer.

Ceterum censeo
A formulaic expression used to end a speech by reinforcing one, often unrelated, major view.

Cha cha
Ballroom dance.

Chain reaction
A series of events, each one causing the next.

Chaise Lounge
Lounge chair.

Chalk up to
To attribute or account for something.

Chalk up
To attribute, credit, or blame.

Champ at the bit
To show impatience at being held back or delayed.

Chance'd be a fine thing
Given to indicate that an aforementioned thing would be desirable but unlikely. Comparable to if I should be so lucky.

Chances are
It is likely that, it is probable that.

Change hands
To become the property of someone else; to be bought or sold.

Change horses in midstream
To change plans or approaches at an inopportune time.

Change of heart
A change of one's opinion, belief or decision.

Change one's mind
To decide differently than one had decided before.

Change one's tune
To reconsider; rethink; to reach a different conclusion.

Chapter and verse
The precise authority backing up a statement or view; established rules for, or detailed information about something.

Charge up
To recharge, to give electrical power to something.

Charity begins at home
Be generous to your family before helping others.

Charity mugger
A person employed by a charity who stands in the street and invites passersby to set up standing orders or direct debits to make regular donations to the charity.

Charley horse
A muscle cramp, usually in the thigh or leg.

Charm the pants off
Very charming.

Charmed life
An existence that appears to be protected by extreme good luck.

Chase a rainbow
To pursue something illusory, impractical, or impossible.

Chase after
To chase someone.

Chase down
To investigate the cause of something.

Chase tail
Partner.

Chat up
To talk in a friendly, open, or casual manner.

Che sera sera
Used to express a personal philosophy of fatalism. "Whatever will be, will be."

Cheap at half the price
Something that is very cheap.

Cheaper by the dozen
Things are handled more efficiently as a group, rather than individually.

Cheat on
To be unfaithful to.

Cheat sheet
Any summary or quick reference used as a shortcut or reminder, a crib sheet.

Cheaters never prosper
One does not gain from cheating.

Check in
To announce or record one's arrival at a hotel, airport etc.

Check is in the mail
A common excuse used by debtors to put off creditors.

Check out
To leave in a hurry.
Cheek by jowl
In close proximity; crammed uncomfortably close together.
Cheer on
To cheer and support a team, to barrack, to root for.
Cheer up
To become happy.
Cheese down
To coil the tail of a rope on deck so as to present a neat appearance.
Cheese it
A minced oath used as a warning to stop, hide, or flee.
Cheese off
To annoy.
Cherry pick
To select only the best from a range of options.
Chew out
To lecture, scold, reprimand, or rebuke.
Chew somebody out
To berate; to shout at someone.
Chew the cud
To meditate or ponder before answering; to be deep in thought; to ruminate.
Chew the fat
To chat idly or generally waste time talking.
Chew the scenery
To display excessive emotion or to act in an exaggerated manner while performing; to be melodramatic; to be flamboyant.

Chicken feed
A very small or insignificant quantity, especially of money.
Chicken out
To shy away from a daring task; to decline, refuse, or avoid something due to fear or uncertainty.
Chickens coming home to roost
Consequences visited upon someone who originally had appeared to escape them.
Child's play
Something particularly simple or easy.
Chill out
Relax, take it easy.
Chime in
To talk; to join in conversation or discussion.
Chin up
Be happy; cheer up.
Chinese gooseberry
Kiwi fruit
Chink in the armor
To have flaw or problem preventing success.
Chip in
To contribute.
Chip off the old block
Someone who takes after their parent.
Chip on one's shoulder
A tendency to take offence quickly.
Chit chat
Gossip
Chomp at the bit
To show impatience or frustration when delayed.

Chopped liver
A person or object which is not worthy of being noticed; someone or something insignificant.

Chow down
To eat, especially to eat vigorously.

Chrome horn
The front bumper of a car when used to bump another vehicle, usually to inform the driver of the other vehicle, that the first car would like to pass.

Chuck away
To discard, or throw away.

Chuck it down
To rain heavily.

Chuck out
To discard, to dispose of.

Chump change
An amount of remuneration, reward, or other monetary recompense considered to be insultingly small.

Circle the wagons
To prepare to defend against an attack.

Circles around
Far faster or better than.

Circuit slugger
A talented baseball batter that hits home runs.

Circular firing squad
A political party or other group experiencing considerable disarray because the members are engaging in internal disputes and mutual recrimination.

Cite chapter and verse
To speak authoritatively, providing detailed factual information.

City slicker
One accustomed to a city or urban lifestyle or unsuited to life in the country.

Claim to fame
That for which one has bragging rights; one's reason for being well-known or famous.

Clam up
To become silent; to stop talking, to shut up.

Clamp down on
To take measures to stop something; to put an end to.

Class clown
A student who frequently makes jokes or pokes fun; a wiseacre.

Clean code
Software code that is formatted correctly and in an organized manner so that another coder can easily read or modify it.

Clean house
To reform by removing undesirable personnel and procedures.

Clean out
To clean, especially to tidy by removing the contents.

Clean someone's clock
To defeat decisively, in a physical fight or other competition or negotiation.

Clean up one's act
To reform; to improve one's habits.

Clean up
To make an area or a thing clean; to pick up a mess; to tidy.

Clear cut
Straightforward, obvious, simple, or basic.

Clear the decks
To prepare for action.

Clear up
To clarify, to correct a misconception.

Climb the walls
To behave in a distressed or frantic manner; to feel very agitated.

Climb up
To make a gradual ascent or increase.

Climbing the walls
Present participle of climb the walls.

Clock in
To begin work.

Clock up
To accumulate a large amount of time or distance.

Clogs to clogs in three generations
Wealth earned in one generation seldom lasts through the third.

Close as wax
Miserly.

Close but no cigar
Almost having reached victory but failing just at the end.

Close down
To surround someone, as to impede their movement.

Close enough for government work
It is not worth investing additional time on perfecting this thing.

Close fisted
Stingy

Close in on
To enclose around; to tighten or shrink; to collapse.

Close off
To seal or block the entrance to a road, an area, or a building so that people cannot enter.

Close one's eyes
To ignore.

Close shave
A near accident or mishap; a dangerous or risky encounter or incident.

Close the stable door after the horse has bolted
To attempt to prevent a problem only to find it has already happened.

Close to home
Affecting people close to, or within, ones family circle.

Close up shop
To shut down a shop; to end a business activity.

Close up
To move people closer together.

Closed book
A person or thing that cannot be easily understood; someone or something incomprehensible or puzzling.

Cloud nine
A state of happiness, elation or bliss; often used in the phrase on cloud nine.

Cloud up
To become cloudy.

Clout list
A usually secret list containing the names of people who are to be given special access, benefits, or influence.

Clue in
To inform, instruct, or tell.

Clue stick
A metaphorical stick used to beat information or understanding into a slow learner.

Clutter up
To fill with rubbish.

Coals to newcastle
A pointless venture, in the sense of sending something to a place where it's made, or where they already have an abundance.

Cock a hoop
Elated.

Cock a snook
To spread one hand, place the thumb on the nose and wriggle some of the fingers as a gesture of disrespect.

Cock of the walk
A proud or conceited person.

Cock up
Mess up.

Cock-and-bull story
A far-fetched and fanciful story or tale of highly dubious validity.

Cockney slang
London slang.

Cold comfort
Much less reassurance, consolation, aid, or pleasure than one needs or desires.

Cold fish
A heartless individual; a person lacking empathy and emotion.

Cold hands, warm heart
Implies inner beauty; a caring person; warm-hearted

Cold one
A beer.

Cold shoulder
A deliberate act of disrespect; a slight or snub.

Cold snap
A period of exceptionally cold weather.

Cold turkey
The physiological effects of such a withdrawal.

Collect dust
To remain untouched and unused for a long period of time.

Collect one's thoughts
To become mentally composed.

Colt over the fence
An illegitimate child.

Combine harvester
Farm vehicle

Come a cropper
To suffer some misfortune; to fail.

Come about
To come to pass; to develop; to occur; to take place; to happen.

Come across
To find, usually by accident.
Come along
To accompany.
Come around
To change one's mind.
Come back
To return to a place.
Come by
To obtain; to get, now especially by chance or involuntarily.
Cry over spilt milk
Don't worry about something that has already happened.

Cry wolf
Lying and asking for help when it is not required .
Cup of Joe
American nickname for a cup of coffee.
Curiosity killed the cat
Don't interfere in others' matters as it will bring harm to you later.
Cut the mustard
Fulfilling standards.
Cut to the chase
Come to the main point of significance.

D

Down to earth
Humble.

Down to the wire
Situation where the result is decided only in the last few seconds.

Drawing a blank
Failing to remember something.

Drive someone nuts
To irritate or annoy somebody.

Dropping like flies
To die in large numbers.

Drive somebody batty
Drive someone bankers. To annoy someone.

E

Eat my hat
Used to express strong disbelief in something.
Elvis has left the building
Over; complete.
Every last
Each used for emphasis.
Every little helps
Even the smallest things are helpful when towards a goal.
Every man has a price
Everyone can be bribed or corrupted for a certain price.
Every man jack
All the members of a group with no exceptions.
Every nook and cranny
Everywhere.
Every rose has it's thorns
Everything, even if it seems perfect, has faults
Every silver lining has a cloud
Every good situation has the potential to turn bad.
Every time
At each occasion that.
Every which way
All over; in every direction.
Every which where
A more emphatic version of everywhere.

Everybody and his cousin
Everybody; a huge crowd; too many people.
Everybody and their brother
A large number of people; most people.
Everything but the kitchen sink
Almost everything, whether needed or not.
Everything happens for a reason
All events are purposeful.
Evil twin
A duplicate or counterpart of something or someone that acts in a contrary, nefarious, or insidious manner.
Execution style
Resembling an execution; with the victim aware, but unable to defend himself or resist.
Experience is the best teacher
Lessons learned from experience are the most lasting.
Expose oneself
To appear nude in public.
Extract the urine
To mess around, cajole.
Eye candy
A very attractive person or the salient visible physical attributes of same.

Eye for an eye
Compensation for injury caused by a person, in the form of inflicting of an identical injury on that person.

Eye of the beholder
The evaluation depending on perception of person who sees and considers.

Eye shadow
Cosmetic item

Eye up
To examine closely something coveted.

F

Fight fire with fire
To return an attack that is similar to the attack used on you.
Fish out of water
Being in an unfamiliar situation.
Fit as a fiddle
To be in perfect health.

Flea market
Market where inexpensive goods are sold.
Foaming at the mouth
To be very angry.
Fool's gold
Iron pyrites, which looks like gold, but is worthless.

G

Get down to brass tacks
To look at the basic facts.
Go by the board
To be finished with
Go for broke
To risk everything.
Go off the boil
To lose interest; to pall.
Go on strike
Take industrial action
Go on the rampage
To behave violently or to riot.
Go on
To continue; expand upon.
Go out of one's way
To make an extra effort.
Go out on a limb
To take a risk.
Go out on the town
To party all night long.
Go out the window
To vanish or cease, especially due to lack of care, attention, etc.; to be discarded, disregarded, or ignored.
Go out with
To date; be involved in a romantic relationship with.
Go out
To leave.

Go over
To look at carefully; to scrutinize; to analyze.
Go overboard
Go too far, be excessive.
Go places
To make progress or achieve success.
Go public
Make public, announce publicly or to the press.
Go red
To become sunburnt/blush.
Go round in circles
To repeatedly do the same thing; without making any progress.
Go south
To become unfavorable; to decrease; to take a turn for the worse.
Go the distance
To have the endurance to see a difficult sustained challenge to its natural end without faltering.
Go the extra mile
To make an extra effort; to do a particularly good job.
Go the way of the dinosaurs/dodo
To go extinct or become obsolete; to fall out of common use or practice; to go off the firsthand market; to become a thing of the past.

Go the way of
To end up the same way as. To receive the same fate as.

Go the whole hog
To do something as entirely or completely as possible; to reserve or hold back nothing.

Go through hell
To have a miserable experience.

Go through the mill
To experience the suffering or discipline necessary to bring one to a certain degree of knowledge or skill, or to a certain mental state.

Go through with
To proceed; to continue.

Go to canossa
To submit to the pope.

Go to pot
To come to a bad end.

Go to seed
To deteriorate; to decline into an unkempt or debased condition.

Go to sleep
An expression used to dismiss an extremely foolish statement, or to dismiss somebody that one does not feel like talking to.

Go to someone's head
To strongly affect a person, especially to the detriment of their senses or mental faculties.

Go to the dogs
To decline or deteriorate.

Go to the mat
To continue to struggle or fight until either victorious or defeated.

Goody two-shoes
A person who is complacently good.

Greased lightning
Very fast.

Gut feeling
Intuition

Hands down
 Easy; certain.
Hard pill to swallow
 Difficult to accept
Head over heels
 Excited.

Heads up
 Prior warning.
Hear, hear
 Said to catch someone's attention.
High and dry
 Abandoned.

I

I smell a rat
Said when something does not feel right.
Ice cream
Dessert item
Ice over
To become covered in ice, usually of a body of water.
Ice up
To become clogged with ice, usually of a mechanical device.
Idiot box
Television.
Idiot light
Any warning light or indicator on the dashboard of a car, designed to alert the driver of problems.
Idiot mittens
Mittens connected by yarn or string running through one sleeve, along the back and out the other sleeve of a coat, to prevent the mittens becoming lost. Generally worn by small children.
If it's all the same
If it makes no difference; if nobody minds; if it doesn't bother anyone.
If looks could kill
A phrase said upon catching sight of someone's giving you a particularly nasty look of discontent or disapproval.
If need be
If necessary; if there is a need.
If only
I wish that; signifies a wish or desire.
If pigs had wings they would fly
Expresses speakers skepticism toward a hypothetical argument by another.
If pigs had wings
Never.
If the shoe fits
If it has all of the characteristics of a thing, it probably is that thing.
If you can't beat them, join them
If your adversaries are stronger than yourself, it is better to join the adversaries.
Ill advisedly
Unwisely
Ill fated
Doomed
Ill health
A state of illness, or bad health.
Ill use
Maltreat
Impiastro
Nuisance, bore.

In a bake
Very angry.
In a bind
In a difficult situation, usually of one's own making; having a dilemma; faced with a problem or a set of problems for which there is no easy solution.
In a bit
Soon.
In a canter
Without much effort; easily.
In a flash
Very quickly.
In a league of one's own
Far excelling even the closest contender; not having any worthy competition.
In a nutshell
In summary; briefly or simply.
In a pig's eye
Very unlikely; probably never.
In a pinch
In an urgent or difficult situation; when no other solution is available.
In a state
Agitated and anxious.
In abraham's bosom
No longer living. Dead.
In addition
Also; as well; besides.
In aid to this fact
In addition to; and furthermore.
In all my born days
Ever.
In all one's glory
Completely naked.
In any way, shape, or form
In any way at all; whatsoever.

In bed with
Engaging in a close mutually beneficial relationship, especially secretly and illicitly.
In bed
Lying on a bed, especially under some bed sheets.
In someone's bad books
To be out of favour with somebody.
In the box-seat
In a superior place.
In the red
In debt.
Into thin air
Immediately and inexplicably out of sight.
Iron out
To resolve.
Is the pope catholic
The answer to the question is, obviously, resoundingly affirmative.
It ain't over 'til the fat lady sings
There are more developments yet to come.
It is easier for a camel to go through the eye of a needle than for a rich man to enter into the kingdom of god
The rich can afford more immoral behavior than the poor.
It is easy to find a stick to beat a dog
If a person is determined to punish someone, they will find a way to do so.
It is not the whistle that pulls the train
Alternative form of it's not the whistle that pulls the train.
It is what it is
This circumstance is simply a fact and must be accepted or dealt with as it exists.

It never rains but it pours
Unfortunate events occur in quantity.
It pays to advertise
Good qualities do not get rewarded automatically.
It takes all kinds to make a world
Diversity is essential.
It takes two to tango
Some things need the active cooperation of two parties; blame is to be laid on both parties in a conflict.
Itchy trigger finger
A tendency to act in haste or without consideration.
It's a long road that has no turning
Encouragement when things are not going well. Just as a long road eventually has a turning, problems also eventually have a solution, even though one might have to wait.
It's about time
Used to express impatience at the eventual occurrence of something that the speaker or writer considered to be long overdue.
It's all good
Used to express unconcern.
It's all greek to me
I don't understand any of it; it makes no sense..
It's all grist to the mill
Everything referred to in the present context has some sort of use.
It's an ill wind that blows nobody any good
There is usually something of benefit to someone, no matter how bad the situation.

It's better to ask forgiveness than permission
The value of acting promptly and making a mistake requiring forgiveness is greater than value of delaying to get permission.
It's not all it's cracked up to be
Not as good as made out to be.
It's not brain surgery
Easy to achieve.
It's not the whistle that pulls the train
Boasting and loud talk should not be mistaken for the work that produces real achievements.
It's not what you know but who you know
For success, and especially to obtain employment, one's knowledge and skills are less useful and less important than one's network of personal contacts.
It's one's funeral
One's decisions or actions will bring undesirable consequences only on oneself.
Itsy bitsy
Minuscule.
Ivory tower
A sheltered, overly-academic existence or perspective, implying a disconnection or lack of awareness of reality or practical considerations.

J

Jack in
To stop doing a regular activity. Often a job or studies.

Jack it in
An imperative to stop doing something that the speaker finds annoying.

Jack of all trades Master of None
Having skills in multiple things, but not being an expert of any.

Jack tar
Nickname for a sailor in the Royal Navy.

Jack up
To raise, increase, or accelerate; often said of prices, fees, or rates. See also jack up the price.

Jaws of Death
Being in a dangerous situation.

Jet set
A set of wealthy people who travel for pleasure.

Jet setting
The actions of the jet set; travelling from one fashionable location to another by jet.

Jet-setter
A member of the jet set, a rich person who travels for pleasure.

Jew down
To bargain or haggle with a seller in order to obtain a lower price for a good or service.

Jig is up
Caught.

Jive turkey
Someone who is jiving, as in behaving in a glib and disingenuous fashion.

Joe job
An uninteresting, low-level, low-paying job.

Join the club
An expression of sympathy for a shared experience.

Join up
To enlist or enroll.

Jolly someone along
To make someone happy or compliant, as by encouragement or flattery.

Jug ears
Ears whose plane is markedly not parallel to the plane of the head.

Jumble sale
Fundraising event

Jumbo jet
Airliner

Jump about
To move from side to side, or fidget annoyingly. Usually as a result of being nervous.

Jump around
To move erratically by jumping. Usually as a result of being excited.

Jump at the chance
To immediately accept an offer.

Jump at
To accept something enthusiastically. Usually an opportunity, or chance, or job etc.

Jump down
To leave an elevated position to a lower position by one jump.

Jump for joy
Exalt.

Jump in one's skin
To start with fright.

Jump in
To enter something quickly. Usually a mode of transport.

Jump off
To move from an elevated place by one jump.

Jump on the bandwagon
To profit from a craze; to join a trend.

Jump on
To attack someone verbally, or criticise them over strongly for small errors.

Jump rope
A single jump in this game or activity, counted as a measure of achievement.

Jump
To attack suddenly and violently.

Jumping the Gun
Beginning too soon.

K

Kangaroo court
A judicial or quasi-judicial proceeding, or a group which conducts such proceedings, which is without proper authority, abusive, or otherwise unjust.

Keel over
To collapse in a faint; to black out; to die.

Keep a close watch on
To pay careful attention to a situation or a thing, so that you can deal with any changes or problems.

Keep a lid on
To keep something secret.

Keep a weather eye open
To be alert; to concentrate on a matter in hand.

Keep an eye on
To watch and pay attention to.

Keep an eye open
To maintain vigilance for a possibly dangerous situation.

Keep an eye peeled
To look out attentively.

Keep at
To persist in.

Keep away from
To avoid.

Keep buggin on
Never quit; go on

Keep down
Repress; Prevent.

Keep from
Protect.

Keep it down
Be quiet.

Keep it real
Be authentic.

Keep it up
To maintain a positive streak.

Keep mum
Be silent (about a secret etc.)

Keep on truckin'
Keep going, don't stop.

Keep on
Persist.

Keep one on one's toes
To be active.

Keep one's cards close to one's chest
Avoid revealing your plans.

Keep one's cool
To remain composed and calm.

Keep one's eye on the ball
To concentrate.

Keep one's eyes peeled
Watch closely.
Keep one's lips sealed
Keep quiet.
Keep one's mouth shut
Keep a secret.
Keep one's options open
To not commit to one single decision.
Keep one's pecker up
Stay cheerful.
Keep oneself to oneself
To stay away from others.
Keep out of
To stay away from...
Keep out
To stay out of a place.
Keep your eyes peeled
Be careful, pay attention.
Keep your shirt on
Be calm.
Knock for a loop
To astonish; to surprise very much.
Knock it off
Stop doing something; desist.
Knock off
An imitation, especially one of poorer quality.
Knock on wood
To take a customary action to ward off some misfortune that is believed to be attracted my a presumptuous statement.
Knock out of the box
To cause something to be replaced by something else.

Knock out
To complete, especially in haste; knock off.
Knock over
To rob; to stage a heist.
Knock somebody's socks off
To impress greatly; amaze; stun.
Knock the living daylights out of
To knock out; to hit and cause to be unconscious.
Knock together
To assemble something quickly; to knock up.
Knock up
To exhaust; wear out; weary; beat; tire out; to fatigue until unable to do more.
Knock your socks off
Surprised.
Knocked for a six
To be defeated; outwitted; outfoxed; beaten
Knocked up
"pregnant", typically outside of marriage.
Knocking on heaven's door
Dying, close to death.
Knock-on effect
A secondary, often unintended effect.
Know like the back of one's hand
To be intimately knowledgeable about something, especially a place.
Know something inside and out
To know something very thoroughly.
Know the ropes
Understanding of how something works.

Know the score
Be aware of a situation, especially of the consequences of misconduct.

Knowledge is power
With knowledge and/or education, one's potential or ability to succeed in the pursuit of his objectives will certainly increase.

Knuckle down
To get to work; to focus on a task.

Knuckle dragger
A large, strong, and rather dimwitted person.

Knuckle sandwich
A punch to the face, especially to the mouth.

Knuckle under
To yield or cooperate when pressured or forced to do so.

L

Let her rip
Go faster.
Lickety split
Be fast; don't delay.
Like billy-O
An extreme standard of comparison
Like father like son
Having the characteristics of one's parent(s).

Long in the tooth
Old in age.
Love birds
A couple in love.
Lovey dovey
Acts of love such as kissing, cuddling and hugging.

Make a bee-line for
To go towards something directly.
Making a scene
Being dramatic and garnering unwanted attention.
Man of few words
A wise person who speaks only when required.

Mountain out of a molehill
Creating an issue about something that is of little significance.
Mouth-watering
Delicious; yummy.
My cup of tea
Matching to one's tastes and habits.

N

Nail biter
A nervous or uncomfortable situation.
Nail down
Firm or certain.
Name and shame
So as to single them out for individual blame and censure.
Narrow down
Make more specific.
Nary a
Not one; none.
National insurance
State social-security scheme
Near miss
Narrowly avoided accident
Near the knuckle
On the Border of acceptability.
Nearly never bulled a cow
Near enough is not good enough.
Neck and neck
Very close in progress, as in a race or contest.
Neck of the woods
A local neighbourhood or region.
Necktie party
An execution by hanging, especially a lynching.

Needle in a haystack
Something that is difficult or impossible to locate; something impossibly complex or intractable.
Ne'er do well
Useless
Neither fish nor fowl
Said of something not easily categorized or not fitting neatly into any established group.
Neither here nor there
Not important; having no significance or influence on the question at hand; not related; not relevant; not germane; not pertinent.
Nervous hit
A production which receives generally favorably notice, but is not assured of success.
Nest egg
A savings; a reserve of money.
Never change a running system
Don't change something that is working
Never in a million years
Absolutely not.
Never in a month of sundays
At no time whatsoever.

Never mind
Do not be concerned.

Never you mind
Do not concern yourself with it; it is none of your business.

New message
Messages coming to the inbox

New school
A style, way of thinking, or method for accomplishing a task that is typical of the current era, as opposed to former eras.

Next to
Almost; nearly.

Nice guy
An adult male who seeks sexual attraction and romantic intimacy, but only finds cordial friendship and platonic love.

Nickel and dime
Small time; operating on a small scale; involving small amounts of money; petty or cheap.

Night owl
One who stays up late at night or goes to bed late.

Night person
A person whose preference or custom is to remain awake and active during the night and the early morning hours, and who usually sleeps during part of the daytime.

Nightcap
A beverage drunk before bed that is usually alcoholic.

No ifs, ands, or buts
To do something without making excuses.

No questions asked
Complete a task without giving excuses.

No-brainer
Very easy; requiring little mental effort.

Not my cup of tea
Not matching one's tastes and habits.

Not the sharpest tool in the shed
Someone who isn't very smart.

O

Off one's base
Crazy.
Old one-two
Paying attention.
On cloud nine
Very happy.

On the ropes
In a hopeless situation.
On the same page
To think similarly.
On your beam ends
To be in a bad situation.

P, Q

Pack away
To store.
Pack up
To move one's residence.
Packing heat
Hiding firearms on oneself.
Pain in the butt
A nuisance.
Pain in the neck
Someone or something irritating.
Paint oneself into a corner
To create a problem for oneself.
Paint the town red
To party wildly.
Paint with a broad brush
To describe objects or phenomenon in general terms.
Painting rocks
Pointless work organised by the government.
Palm off
To attempt to pass off a counterfeit product as genuine.
Pan out
To succeed.

Paper trail
A written record.
Par for the course
Usual.
Parcel out
To divide into portions.
Pardon me
Sorry; please repeat what you said.
Pardon my french
Please excuse my bad language.
Pare down
To reduce gradually.
Parking lot
An open area where automobiles are left when not in use.
Part and parcel
That which is accepted as part of something else.
Parting shot
An insult said as the conversation ends.
Party animal
A person who parties frequently.
Party crasher
Someone who attempts to enter a party without an invite.

Party pooper
Someone who ruins the fun.
Party to
Having knowledge of.
Playing for keeps
Things are getting serious.
Playing possum
Pretending to be dead.
Plot thickens
A situation that has become more difficult.

Poke fun at
Make fun of.
Put a sock in it
Be quiet.
Quality time
Spending time with someone to strengthen/improve the relationship.
Quick and dirty
Doing things fast may ruin them eventually.
Quick on the draw
Doing something really fast.

R

Rabble rouser
Someone or something that tends to inspire mobs; something controversial or provocative.

Rack one's brain
To struggle to think of or remember something.

Rag bagger
A sailor who tends to sail on messy cruising vessels.

Rag the puck
To proceed slowly at any activity in order to use up time; to stall for time.

Rag-chewing
A phrase used by morse code operators for a longer than usual conversation, generally a conversation extending about 30 minutes.

Rags to riches
In a biographical context, from poverty to exceptional wealth.

Rain cats and dogs
To rain very heavily.

Rain check
To provide a service at a later date.

Rain on someone's parade
To disappoint or discourage someone.

Rain on your parade
To spoil a situation.

Rain or shine
Regardless of what the circumstances are, and how the weather is.

Rain pitchforks
To rain heavily.

Raining cats and dogs
Raining heavily.

Rainy day
A difficult period of need, when things do not go right.

Raise a hand
To volunteer.

Raise a stink
To complain; to demand attention or remedy for a problem.

Raise cain
To cause trouble.

Raise hell
To cause a great disturbance.

Raise one's hand
To dare to question.

Raise somebody's hackles
Make someone angry.

Raise the bar
To raise standards or expectations, especially by creating something to a higher standard.

Raise the flag and see who salutes
To float an idea to see what response or controversy it generates usually as preliminary step.

Raise the spectre
To cause concern that something unfortunate might happen.

Raise the stakes
To increase in significance or risk.

Rake
A lot, plenty.

Ramp up
To increase rapidly to a new value.

Rank and file
Those lacking any particular title or status; those having no station.

Raring to go
Extremely eager or anxious to begin.

Rat race
An activity or situation which is congested with participants and which is hectic or tedious, especially in the context of a busy, modern urban lifestyle.

Rat run
A small road that people venture down when they want to sneak off the motorway and take a short cut.

Rattle off
To list or recite quickly.

Rattle someone's cage
To demand attention; to nag, nudge, or remind.

Re-run
Repeat

Reach an early grave
To resign near the start, for good.

Reach for the stars
To have high hopes, to be ambitious.

Read between the lines
To infer a meaning that is not stated explicitly.

Read 'em and weep
Said by the winner in poker.

Read lips
To lip-read.

Read out
To read something and say the words to inform other people.

Read somebody the riot act
To scold or berate somebody; to reprimand.

Read somebody's lips
To discern what somebody is saying by watching the shape of the mouth rather than by hearing the sounds of the words.

Real deal
A thing or person which is genuine, authentic, or worthy of serious regard.

Real job
A job that can't be replaced advantageously by a machine or a procedure.

Real mckoy
The genuine thing, neither a substitute nor an imitation.

Reality check
A wake-up call, reminder.

Rebound relationship
A relationship proceeding a longterm relationship, usually short in duration and used to help mend the "broken heart".

Rebrousser chemin
To retrace one's steps, to turn back.

Reckon for
To answer for; to pay the account for.
Reckon on
To plan on; to expect.
Reckon upon
To count upon or depend upon.
Reckon with
To deal with.
Reckon without
To ignore that which cannot readily be ignored.
Red face test
A hypothetical test of a person's embarrassment.
Red flag
A cue, warning, or alert; a sign or signal that something is wrong.
Red herring
A clue that is misleading or that has been falsified, intended to divert attention.
Red-hot
Very exciting or successful.
Red ink
A euphemism for financial loss.
Red letter day
Important or happy occasion.
Red light
A warning to stop.
Red mist
Anger sufficient to cloud judgement, to stop clear thinking.
Ride him, cowboy!
A phrase used to cheer cowboys in rodeos.
Right off the bat
Immediately.
Roll with the punches
To endure.

Rub up against
To touch a person's body in a friendly manner, seeking attention.
Rubber-chicken dinner
A formal dinner or event thrown by politicians to raise funds.
Rubbish dump
Tip
Ruffle some feathers
To disturb; to arouse resentment, anger, or concern.
Rugby league
Sport
Rule of thumb
A general guideline, rather than a strict rule; an approximate measure or means of reckoning based on experience or common knowledge.
Rule out
To cross an item out by drawing a straight line through it, as with a ruler.
Rule with an iron fist
To rule with absolute authority or to the detriment of the people. To rule tyrannically.
Rules ok
To be popularly accepted, or supported by the general majority of people.
Rum go
An odd affair; a surprising event; a confusing experience; a queer thing.
Rumor campaign
A method of persuasion in which damaging rumors or innuendo are deliberately spread concerning a person or other target, while the source of the rumors tries to avoid detection.

Rumor mill
A group or network of persons who originate or promulgate gossip and other unsubstantiated claims.

Run a bath
To fill a bathtub with water in preparation for taking a bath.

Run a mile
To escape, flee or leave a situation or relationship, usually as a result of a shocking or sudden announcement or revelation.

Run across
To find or discover by chance.

Run afoul of
To become entangled in; to run aground on.

Run after
To make a determined effort to win someone's affections.

Run along
To leave.

Run around after
To spend a lot of time doing things for another person or group of people. Often used when that person could reasonably do the things for themselves.

Run around/about
To be very busy doing many different things.

Run away with
To be misled by imagining that one's desires can come true.

Run away
To flee by running.

Run back
To rewind a film or cassette.

Run by
To inform someone briefly of the main points of an idea.

Run down
To criticize someone or an organisation, often unfairly.

Run for office
To seek political power.

Run for one's money
A difficult challenge for the person indicated, especially one involving a competitive situation.

Run for the hills
Flee.

Run for the roses
A hard-fought competition or demanding challenge of any kind.

Run for
To try to obtain political position through the democratic voting process.

S

Sabre-rattling
 A flamboyant display of military power as an implied threat that it might be used.
Sack out
 To fall asleep, usually from implied exhaustion.
Sacred cow
 Something which cannot be tampered with, or criticized, for fear of public outcry.
Safe and sound
 Having come to no harm, especially after being exposed to danger.
Safety pin
 Fastener
Said and done
 Agreed to and accomplished or finished.
Sainted
 Simple past tense and past participle of saint.
Salad years
 The inexperienced, youthful prime of an individual, group, organization or entity.
Salmon pink
 Colour

Same difference
 It makes no difference; it amounts to the same thing.
Same old story
 What usually happens, a happening which is not surprising.
Sauce for the goose
 A short form of what's sauce for the goose is sauce for the gander
Save face
 To take an action or make a gesture intended to preserve one's reputation or honour.
Save someone's bacon
 To save someone's life.
Save the day
 To rescue the situation.
Saw wood
 To snore loudly.
Say goodbye
 To separate from someone.
Say grace
 To recite a prayer of invocation or thanksgiving at meal time.
Scare out of one's wits
 To frighten someone to such an extent that they behave irrationally.

Scare the bejeebers out of
To thoroughly terrify.
Scare the pants off of
To scare or startle thoroughly.
Scared shitless
Very scared, terrified.
Scared to death
Extremely frightened.
Scarf down
To eat something quickly.
School of hard knocks
An education consisting of real-world experiences, especially harsh experiences.
Scissor bill
Someone considered contemptible or foolish.
Scope out
To examine; to scout; to investigate; to check out.
Scotch mist
Fine rain
Scot-free
Released from custody.
Scrape off
To remove something by a scraping action.
Scrape the bottom of the barrel
To use the least desirable parts of something.
Scrape through
To marginally manage to progress.
Scrape together
To collect, assemble or gather small amounts, from various sources, with some difficulty.
Scratch one's head
To puzzle, ponder, or wonder about something.
Scratch that
To disregard, omit, or ignore the previous statement.
Scratch the surface
To barely begin; to see or do only a fraction of what is possible.
Screen out
To exclude.
Screen test
Movie audition
Screw back
To cue the cue ball in such a way as to impart backspin. On impact, the ball will follow a reverse trajectory according to the spin.
Screw it
Whatever.
Seeing eye to eye
To agree.
Short end of the stick
Not getting a desired outcome, usually the least desired.
Shot in the dark
An attempt that has little chance of success.
So a fool repeats his folly
Foolish people repeatedly do foolish things.
Son of a gun
Refers to a person, usually one who is behaving badly.

T

Talk the talk
Supporting what you say, not just with words, but also through action or evidence.

That ring any bells?
Recalling a memory; causing a person to remember something or someone.

The back of beyond
A lonely deserted place.

The balance of power
An equal distribution of power.

The balance of trade
It is the difference between the value of a nation's imports and exports.

The big apple
A term for New York.

The big cheese
Most important person.

The bitter end
Reaching one's limit.

The blind leading the blind
Referring to someone who is incompetent who leads similarly incompetent people.

The buck stops here
Responsibility should be taken at this point and not passed on to others.

Throw in the towel
Giving up; to surrender.

Top drawer
High quality, exceptional; something that's very valuable.

Tough it out
To remain resillient even in hard times; enduring.

Tug of war
It can refer to the popular rope pulling game or it can mean a struggle for authority.

Two down, one to go
Two things have been completed, but there is one more that has yet to be finished.

U

Ugly duckling
One who might seem plain at first in appearance or capability, but later turns out to be quite beautiful and spectacular.
Uncle sam
Referring to the U.S. government
Under a cloud
Under suspicion.
Under a spell
Bewitched.
Under fire
Held responsible.
Under fire
Open to enemy attack.
Under lock and key
Imprisoned.
Under one's belt
Practiced.
Under one's breath
Speaking softly.
Under one's hat
Confidential.
Under one's nose
Obvious.
Under one's nose
Visible.
Under one's thumb
Controlled by someone.

Under one's wing
Under one's protection or mentorship.
Under pressure
Subjected to pressure- either physical or emotional.
Under sail
Powered by the wind.
Under the gun
Under pressure to perform.
Under the impression
Making wrong assumptions.
Under the influence
Intoxicated.
Under the knife
Undergoing surgery.
Under the microscope
Under close scrutiny.
Under the radar
In a secretive manner.
Under the table
Secretly
Under the Weather
Not feeling well, in health or mood.
Under the wire
At the last minute.
Under the yoke
To be enslaved.

Under way
In progress.
Under wraps
Secret.
Under your nose
Missing something that should be really obvious.
Underwater basket weaving
An easy and useless class.
University of life
The real world as guidance.
Unring a bell
To perform the impossible; to reverse the irreversible.
Until hell freezes over
Forever
Until one is blue in the face
Forever; for a hopelessly long time.
Until the cows come home
For a very long time.
Unwashed masses
People who are considered uneducated and uncivilized.
Up a creek
In trouble; in a difficult situation.
Up against
Facing; challenging, or opposing.
Up for
Planned; next in line.
Up in arms
Angry; being roused to the point that you are ready to fight.
Upsy daisy
This is said when lifting a baby upwards.

V

Valley of death
Death; or a place or period where death is impending.

Valley of the shadow of death
Valleys on earth one must walk through, that is, part of the human experience.

Variety is the spice of life
Variety is what makes life interesting.

Verge on
To approach or come close to something; to border or be on the edge of something.

Vertically challenged
Of a person, short.

Vice squad
Police department.

Victory at sea
Ocean conditions very windblown and messy, possibly to the point of being inimical to surfing and other water sports.

Virgin territory
Land that has never been explored or developed.

Vote down
By a majority vote.

Vote in
To collectively approve a nominee into an office or position as a result of voting.

Vote out
To expel the holder of an office or other position through an act of voting.

Vote with one's feet
To show a lack of support for something by departing or otherwise absenting oneself.

Vouch for
To affirm the truth or reliability of.

Wack out
To become deranged.

Wade in
To interrupt someone, or a situation, by doing or saying something abruptly, or forcefully, and usually without thinking about the consequences.

Wade through
To do a boring, repetitive research task.

Wage war
A figurative allusion to pay discrepancies.

Wail on
To beat heavily on anything.

Wait for the other shoe to drop
To await a seemingly inevitable event, especially one which is not desirable.

Wait up
Wait.

Wake up and smell the coffee
To face reality and stop deluding oneself.

Wake up call
A warning or some type of occurance that brings a problem to somebody's attention, and they realize it needs to be fixed right away.

Wake up on the wrong side of bed
To feel grumpy, irritable; to be easily annoyed.

Walk a tightrope
To undertake a precarious course of action.

Walk and chew gum at the same time
To do something very easy.

Walk around
To walk with no real planned destination, but to just walk, to meander "around".

Walk away from
To abandon or leave; to shun.

Walk in on
To enter suddenly or unexpectedly while something is happening; to intrude or interrupt by entering.

Walk in the park
Something easy or pleasant, especially by comparison to something.

Walk in the snow
An occasion when a momentous career decision is made, especially a decision to resign or retire.

Walk into
Meet with unwittingly.

Walk it off
To deal with an negative emotional event without complaint.
Walk on eggshells
To be careful and sensitive in handling very sensitive matters.
Walk out on
To abandon or desert someone, especially a spouse.
Walk out
To stage a walkout or strike.
Walk the line
To behave in an authorized or socially accepted manner, especially as prescribed by law or morality; to exercise self-control.
Walk the plank
To be forced to resign from a position in an organization.
Walk the talk
To do what one said one could do, or would do, not just making empty promises. To walk one's talk is to be innocent of hypocrisy.
Walk the walk
Act competently, like an expert.
Walked out on
To abandoned; to desert
Walking on air
Very happy

Wall in
To enclose by surrounding with walls.
Wall off
To separate with a wall.
Wall to wall carpets
Floor coverings
Wall up
To seal with a wall.
Walls have ears
There is a risk of being heard, so pay attention to what you say.
War bride
A company or individual whose business is increased by warfare.
What am I, chopped liver?
A rhetorical question used by a person who feels they are being given less attention or consideration than someone else.
When the rubber hits the road
When something is about to begin, get serious, or be put to the test.
Wild goose chase
Futilely pursuing something that will never be attainable.
Wouldn't harm a fly
Nonviolent; someone who is mild or gentle.
Wouldn't touch with a barge-pole
Referring to something that no one would even go near to.

Y

Yada yada
A way to notify a person that what they're saying is predictable or boring.

Yak shaving
Any apparently useless activity which, by allowing you to overcome intermediate difficulties, allows you to solve a larger problem.

Yank off
To remove something, like a piece of cloth or bread, by tearing it with one quick strong pull.

Yank out
To remove something like a nail, or a tooth with one quick strong pull.

Year dot
A very long time ago, from the beginning or as far back as one can remember.

Year in, year out
During every year; always.

Yell at
To scold, to rebuke - often by yelling.

Yell silently
To think very strong thoughts, that one wishes to yell out loud but does not.

Yellow journalism
Material published in a broadcast or periodical, such as a tabloid newspaper or magazine, which is sensationalistic and of questionable accuracy and taste.

Yellow light
Limited approval or permission to proceed.

Yellow press
Newspapers which publish sensationalist articles rather than well researched and sober journalism.

Yellow-bellied
Uncourageous.

Yes man
A person who always agrees with his employer or superior.

Yes to death
To agree with someone, often sarcastically.

Yes-man
A person of unquestioning obedience.

Yield up
To give something against one's will.

Yoke together
To unite, or join, or combine.

You and whose army
You can't do all that on your own.
You are what you eat
If you eat well, you will be well; but if you eat badly you will feel bad.
You bet
Certainly; you're welcome; a reply to thank you or to a request.
You can hang your hat on that
It's something to put faith in, to rely upon or trust.
You can say that again
That is very true.
You can't fight city hall
Nothing can be done to change the situation, because it is a governmental decision.
You can't get a quart into a pint pot
What is being discussed is not possible.

You can't polish a turd
Something inherently bad cannot be improved.
You can't say fairer than that
That is good, reasonable, or fair; one cannot hope for a better decision or outcome.
You can't take it with you
It is not possible to take one's material wealth to whatever world may await one after death.
You don't say really?
No kidding!; is that so? sometimes used sarcastically in response to the obvious
You get more with a kind word and a gun than you do with a kind word alone
It is advantageous not to rely solely on being nice.
You get what you pay for
In commercial transactions, the quality of goods and services increases as the prices increase.

www.ingramcontent.com/pod-product-compliance
Lightning Source LLC
Chambersburg PA
CBHW070337230426
43663CB00011B/2361